Scandinavian Christmas Crafts and Recipes

D1613685

0 11557 01425 9

Helene S. Lundberg

Scandinavian Christmas Crafts and Recipes

STACKPOLE
BOOKS

Copyright © 2014 by Stackpole Books
Original Norwegian edition, *Julefryd*, copyright © 2009 by
CAPPELEN DAMM AS

Published by
STACKPOLE BOOKS
5067 Ritter Road
Mechanicsburg, PA 17055
www.stackpolebooks.com

All rights reserved, including the right to reproduce this book
or portions thereof in any form or by any means, electronic or
mechanical, including recording or by any information storage
and retrieval system, without permission in writing from the
publisher. All inquiries should be addressed to Stackpole Books,
5067 Ritter Road, Mechanicsburg, PA 17055.

The contents of this book are for personal use only. Patterns
contained herein may be reproduced in limited quantities for such
use. Any large-scale commercial reproduction is prohibited without
the written consent of the publisher.

Printed in the United States of America
10 9 8 7 6 5 4 3 2 1
First edition

Translator: Toril Blomquist
All projects and drawings: Helene S. Lundberg
Photos: Helene S. Lundberg
Interior design: Laila S. Gundersen
Cover design: Tessa J. Sweigert

Library of Congress Cataloging-in-Publication Data

Lundberg, Helene S., author.
    [Julefryd. English]
    Scandinavian Christmas crafts and recipes / Helene S. Lundberg. —
First edition.
        pages cm
    ISBN 978-0-8117-1425-9
    1. Christmas decorations.   2. Christmas cooking.   I. Title.
    TT900.C4L96413 2014
    745.594'12—dc23
                                                    2014019844

Contents

Preface

Christmas is the holiday and time of year I appreciate most. I think
the whole month of December is wonderful. And the weeks before
Christmas—otherwise known as Advent—are almost better than Christmas
Eve itself. That's when all the charming and traditional preparation
happens. I appreciate both small and big experiences, from lighting the
first Advent candle to watching the Saint Lucy's Day procession with little
girls and boys holding candles, to eating saffron buns and everything else
that comes with this time—not to mention all the beautiful Christmas lighting
that pops up in gardens and windows.

A visit to a Christmas market and the opening of your main street for
Christmas are also nice occasions for soaking up some happy, old-
fashioned Christmas spirit. The first gingerbread cookies and mulled wine
of the year should be enjoyed outdoors at a Christmas market, surrounded
by happy children, a crackling fire, and live music. Christmas is the time to
nurture friendships and spend as much time as possible with your nearest
and dearest. Don't plan to do or attend too much before Christmas;
instead choose the things you really enjoy doing. You have to put aside
some time for some Christmas crafting, after all! The holiday is made so
much more charming and fun by little homemade presents and surprises,
and I can promise you that they will be more appreciated than any store-
bought present. I hope this book will inspire you to make something tasty,
something pretty, and something new this Christmas.

And don't forget that Christmas is supposed to be a nice and relaxing time
for the family—not for commercialized hype!

A merry and peaceful Christmas is wished for you all!

Helene

Sew and Embroider

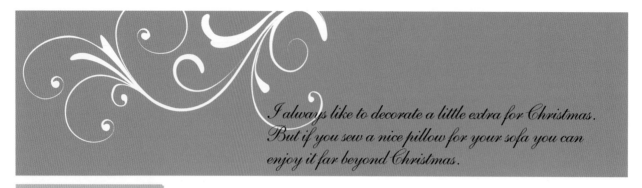

I always like to decorate a little extra for Christmas. But if you sew a nice pillow for your sofa you can enjoy it far beyond Christmas.

Materials

* Pattern and tracing paper
* Natural- and beige-colored linen
* Striped cotton fabric
* Red yarn
* Small, pearl-colored glass beads
* Pearl buttons
* Red yarn or finished red pom-poms
* Fiberfill or pillow form
* Sewing machine, needle, pins
* Scissors
* Disappearing-ink fabric marker

Here I've mixed and matched clean linen with striped cotton, then embroidered a bead-and-button heart and sewn pom-poms along the short sides. I think it turned out to be a very successful mix. The pillow gives the impression of being new and modern while retaining an old-fashioned charm.

Pillow with Pom-Poms

The heart is fairly easy to embroider using stem stitching. When traced from the pattern, it's something everyone can do. Attach some buttons and beads to the heart, like you see in the picture. Finished pom-poms can be bought in crafting supply stores, but you can of course also make them yourself.

SEWING THE FRONT PIECE:

* Cut out the pieces for the pillow: two 6 x 12-in. (15 x 30 cm) pieces of the white linen and two 12 x 14-in. (30 x 35 cm) pieces of the beige linen. Zigzag around the edges.
* Transfer the heart pattern from page 116 onto the white linen, and embroider stem stitches using red yarn. As you embroider, remember to attach the beads at all four tips of the crosses. Place the embroidery between damp cloths (you may use an iron and apply very gentle pressure to it) so it becomes straight.
* Attach the buttons with regular thread in a matching color.

* Pin and sew the striped pieces, right side to right side, to the embroidered middle piece. Press the seam open and sew a seam on the right side, ¼ in. (0.6 cm) from the seam.

SEWING THE BACK PIECE:

* Fold in the short sides of the beige fabric 1 in. (2.5 cm), and attach the fold with a seam.
* Let the pieces of the back overlap each other and place them right side to right side with the front piece. Pin and sew the pillow together.
* Reverse the pillow to the right side, push out the corners, and press along the edges.
* Sew on the pom-poms by hand along the short sides.
* Stuff the pillow with fiberfill or use a foam pillow form. If you choose fiberfill you should stitch up the opening in the back by hand.

Don't leave Christmas cards lying around—collect them in a handmade Christmas card pocket. I've created a few different options to choose from.

Heart-Shaped Pocket for Christmas Cards

Materials

* Pattern and tracing paper
* Gray wadmal or other thick wool fabric
* Light gray perle cotton
* Sewing needle and pins
* Button
* Scissors and a pen
* Disappearing-ink fabric marker or chalk
* Tree branch
* White acrylic paint
* Paintbrush

Isn't this a decorative way to store the Christmas mail? This is a fun project that is easier than it looks. This large, heart-shaped Christmas card pocket is sewn with old-fashioned gray wadmal and hung on a white branch in the hall. With an embroidered snow crystal in light gray perle cotton and a nice pearl-colored button in the middle, it will be a good eye-catcher.

It is best to use a felted fabric that won't fray. I've used wadmal, which is steady and thick and helps keep the heart shape in place.

You can find branches outside. Pick one that fell to the ground during autumn. Bring the branch inside and let it dry well before painting it white. You can hang it on the wall using strong thread, or use fishing line if you want a tie that doesn't show.

DIRECTIONS:

* Trace the pattern from the tracing paper to the fabric.
* Cut out four heart pieces and two handles measuring 1 ½ x 12 in. (4 x 30 cm).
* Draw the snow crystal on the right side of one heart piece, embroider the figure with stem stitching, and sew on the button.
* Place the pieces together and pin. Two heart shapes form each side of the pocket. Attach the two handles between the layers with pins.
* Using perle cotton, tack together the pieces by hand. Reinforce the seam in the transition between the pocket and the opening where it goes from four to two layers.
* Paint a dried branch white and let the paint dry.
* Hang the pocket on the branch and nail it to the wall, or hang it with a strong thread.

Here is a different version, a fabric bag with an attached Christmas tree decorated with shimmering ornaments. It looks nice in all its simplicity, and creates Christmas spirit in the living room.

Materials

* Pattern and tracing paper
* White and green wool fabric
* Green wool yarn
* Ball-shaped buttons, beads, or bells
* Green thread
* Sewing needle and pins
* Scissors and a pen

A Christmas Tree for the Christmas Cards

The small ornaments on this tree are pieces of jewelry that can be found in the crafting supply stores. You may decorate the Christmas tree in gold beads or ball-shaped buttons, or use small bells as ornaments. I dyed the fabric and yarn myself; it is fun to do everything from scratch—and it makes the project a great conversation piece. In this way I got the exact same color for the fabric and the yarn.

I've used wadmal, a felted wool fabric that doesn't fray, but the stitches around the edge will help hold the threads in place even if you use an unfelted material. The pattern for the Christmas tree can be found on page 120, but if you want you can easily make your own version by changing the theme or the colors. A green pocket with a big red heart is an easy alternative.

DIRECTIONS:

* Transfer the pattern of the Christmas tree (page 120) to the green fabric and cut out.
* Cut out a rectangle measuring 18 x 10 in. (46 x 25 cm) from the white fabric.
* Measure out the position, pin the tree to the white fabric, and sew using buttonhole stitching.
* Attach the ball-shaped buttons, beads, or bells to the tree.
* Fold the fabric to create a pocket and sew it together with green wool yarn using buttonhole stitches.
* Sew buttonhole stitches in green on the top along the edges of the pocket.

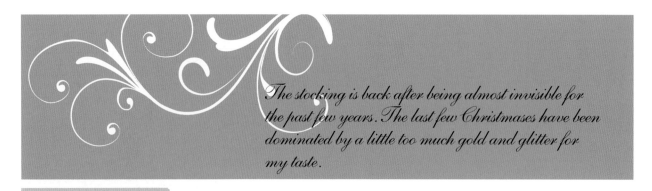

The stocking is back after being almost invisible for the past few years. The last few Christmases have been dominated by a little too much gold and glitter for my taste.

Materials

* Pattern and tracing paper
* White cotton fabric
* Striped cotton fabric
* Fusible web
* Woven cotton ribbon
* Perle cotton in blue and white
* Disappearing-ink fabric marker
* Pen, scissors
* Sewing machine
* Iron
* Sewing needle and pins

Country-Style Stocking

Gold was a trendy crafting color during recent Christmases. Everyone was using gold ribbon with wire in the sides, and everything had a layer of gold spray; candles and ribbon and even the flowers were getting a gold sprinkle! Finally we can enjoy details in delicate and nice colors in combinations that give peace to the mind and soul.

This stocking is my interpretation of English "country style." I think it creates exactly the right feeling, but I realize that not everyone likes the same things I do. Many still want some gold and glitter. Thankfully there is room for finding your own style and you can use exactly the colors and fabrics you like.

Use your leftover fabrics and sew several stockings. Sew one big monogram on each stocking. The simple and decorative stitches are something I like to call "candy cane stitch." If you sew them in red and white they will look like a candy

cane! Here I've used stem stitches in blue yarn cast over with white. It gives a nice effect.

DIRECTIONS:

* Transfer the pattern to the tracing paper and cut out. Pin the pattern to double fabric, trace, and cut out. Zigzag around the edges so they won't fray as you work on the stocking.
* Draw your chosen monogram, letter, number, or other figure on the stocking using a disappearing-ink fabric marker. Embroider using stem stitch and perle cotton along the drawn line. Attach on the wrong side. Embroider with the other color around the first stitches.
* Cut out the striped pieces according to the pattern. Iron fusible web to the wrong side (for heel and toes), draw from the pattern, and cut out. Pull off the protective paper backing, place the pieces, and iron them onto the stocking in the style of the picture. Sew a wide and dense zigzag along the edges.

* Pin and sew the striped edge, right side to right side, to the stocking. Press the seam allowance towards the striped piece.
* Place the pieces right side to right side and pin or sew them together using a fairly small seam allowance.
* Fold down the striped edge halfway and pin. Reverse the stocking.
* Cut off a piece of the woven ribbon for a loop, double-fold it, and pin it to the inside of the stocking. Sew two seams, one in the top edge and another one a few millimeters from the seam. In this way you attach the loop while at the same time attaching the fold.

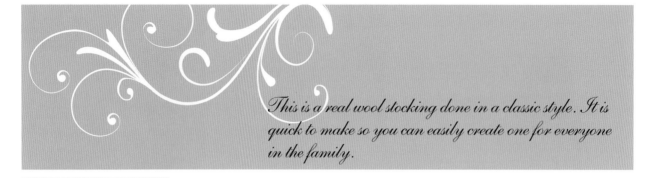

This is a real wool stocking done in a classic style. It is quick to make so you can easily create one for everyone in the family.

Materials

* Patterns and tracing paper
* Gray and red wadmal or other wool fabric (preferably 100 percent wool)
* Loose locks of sheep wool
* Felt needle and base
* Gray and red wool yarn
* Ribbon for loop
* Gray thread
* Scissors, pen, sewing needle, and pins

Classic Stocking in Wool

Try giving away a Christmas present in a stocking like this instead of using the classic wrapping. It's like two presents in one. Attach a big red heart to the stocking, and it would be hard to find someone who wouldn't love to receive this.

Use real sheep's wool to decorate the stocking along the edges, around the whole stocking, or only in the front. You can find sheep's wool in crafting supply stores. Attach the wool with a felting needle. It is fun and easy. Simply press the needle up and down until the wool fibers have attached to the fabric. Remember to place something between the two layers so you don't felt the two pieces together. A piece of Styrofoam works well if you don't have a specially made base for felting.

DIRECTIONS:

* Transfer the pattern pieces from the tracing paper to the wool fabric.
* Cut out two stocking pieces and one heart.
* Pin the heart to the front of the stocking and sew on with buttonhole stitches.
* Pin together the two stocking pieces with the right sides out, and tack them together with even stitches a bit from the edge.
* Place the felting base inside the opening and place locks of wool along the edge. Push the felting needle up and down in the wool so it attaches well to the stocking.
* Attach the ribbon as a loop in the side of the stocking.

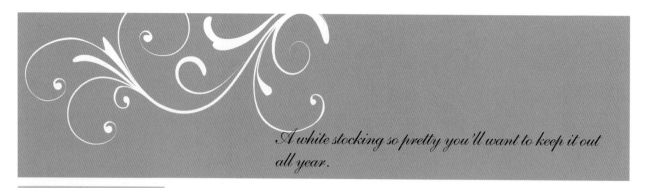

A white stocking so pretty you'll want to keep it out all year.

Materials

* Pattern and tracing paper
* White cotton fabric
* Ribbon with mini pom-poms
* White cotton ribbon (for the loop)
* Transfer paper for the motif
* Scissors, pen
* Pins
* Décor of choice
* Scanner and computer, or copy machine
* Inkjet printer
* Iron
* Sewing machine and matching thread

Christmas Stocking in White

The motif on this piece is a beautiful angel picture transferred and pressed onto the stocking using an iron. The top edge is decorated with a lovely pom-pom ribbon. You can of course change the motif and colors to fit the recipient. With a color switch it can even fit the man of the house! I can easily imagine a green stocking with a design of a moose head. That would be very popular with several guys I know!

When using transfer paper you can use your own digital files, find pictures on the Internet, or scan or copy something you have on paper. Just make sure you don't use a picture that is protected by copyright. Look in your children's storybooks or among your old glossy pictures—you can find many nice, old-fashioned, and romantic pieces.

DIRECTIONS:

* Transfer the pattern pieces to the cotton fabric.
* Cut out two stocking pieces and zigzag around the edges. Pin together right side to right side. Sew together on the wrong side, reverse the stocking, and press the seam open.
* Scan or copy a fitting picture and print it on transfer paper (transfer paper can be found in crafting supply stores or paper shops).
* Cut out the picture, place it on the stocking, and iron it on using a warm iron. Read the instructions for the transfer paper before you start.
* Fold in the edge on top and pin the ribbon with the pom-poms as well as the loop. Attach everything with a seam.

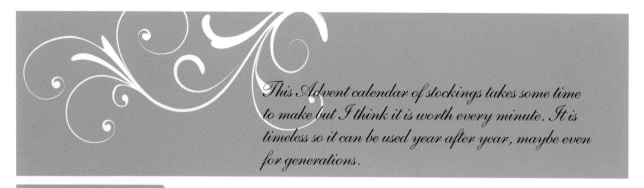

This Advent calendar of stockings takes some time to make but I think it is worth every minute. It is timeless so it can be used year after year, maybe even for generations.

Materials

* Pattern and tracing paper
* Felt in red and white
* Checked cotton fabric
* Fusible web
* Velcro
* Pins
* Tape measure
* Pen, scissors, iron
* Thread and sewing machine
* 2 dowels, ½ in. (1.3 cm) in diameter and 40 in. (102 cm) long
* Red acrylic paint
* Paintbrush
* Perhaps a saw and sandpaper
* Red satin ribbon and bells

Stocking Advent Calendar

The calendar is just as pretty without presents in the stockings, but I guarantee it will be much more appreciated with something *in* the stockings.

Keep to a few colors; here I've used red and winter white with tartan numbers and edges. If you use too many colors, the calendar will be too loud, and may end up dominating the room. That is not the intention—the Christmas tree also needs the attention it deserves! Double-sided fusible web is absolutely necessary for this work. It makes it easier to place the numbers; just iron them on with a hot iron.

DIRECTIONS:

* Transfer the numbers from page 117, or print out numbers from your computer. Remember that the numbers must be reflected.
* Place the fusible web on the numbers and draw the outlines. Press the fusible web to the wrong side of the tartan fabric. Cut out the numbers when they have cooled down.
* Transfer the stocking pattern to the felt fabrics. Cut out 24 red and 24 white pieces.

(Continued on page 23.)

* Peel the protective paper off the numbers and iron them onto the stockings with a hot iron.
* Cut the Velcro into 24 1 in. (2.5 cm) pieces. Sew the loop side halves of the Velcro pieces to the backs of the stockings.
* Place the two pieces together, wrong side to wrong side (right sides out), and sew them together with an even seam a bit from the edge. If you want, you can use a white thread on the red socks and red on the white in order to create a decorative contrast.
* Cut out a piece of felt for the back, 40 x 35 in. (102 x 90 cm). Also cut out the tartan fabric for the edges, two pieces 40 x 4 in. (102 x 10 cm). Attach the edges

to the wrong side on the top and bottom of the back piece, fold in the sides about 1 in. (2.5 cm), and sew a seam. Fold in the tartan edges to create a runner that you can attach with a seam.
* Lay out the socks to find the right places for the hook side halves of the Velcro pieces. Pin the Velcro to the back piece (adjust with a tape measure if necessary) and sew it on using a sewing machine.
* If necessary, saw the sticks to the right length and sand the edges. Paint them red and thread them through the runners when they are dry. Tie satin ribbon to the top stick, and hang the calendar on the wall. Decorate with bells, pom-poms, or tassels (see page 60).

It is very nice to have a few special things to bring out only at Christmas. Here I've made a pillow using an old and classic technique.

Materials

* Pattern
* Tracing paper, transfer pen, and iron
* Wool fabric for front and back sides
* Wool yarn (colors listed below)
* Cotton fabric in matching colors
* Cutting board, metal ruler, rotary cutter
* Pins, sewing needle, and thread
* Sewing machine
* Embroidery needle, scissors, and pen
* Fiberfill or other stuffing

WOOL YARN:
* Gray
* Dark red
* Light red
* Yellow
* Blue
* Green

Small Pillow with Reindeer

The yarn and the embroidery base are made from wool, while the pom-poms in the corners are made from cotton. Pom-poms in the corners like these were normal in embroidery from Skåne (in the south of Sweden) in the old days. At that time they used fabrics that that invoked "special memories" to decorate the corners.

The pillow is sewn in simple embroidery like stem stitching, satin stitch, and French knots. You will get the best result if you use a one-thread wool yarn. When the work is done, you should place it between damp pieces of fabric with some pressure on it and leave it for two days. This will make the work straight and nice while keeping the volume. An iron will often press the embroidery too much, even with something soft underneath.

DIRECTIONS:
* Cut the front and back pieces, about 14 x 14 in. (36 x 36 cm).
* Trace the pattern from page 119 onto the fabric using the transfer pen. Read the pen manufacturer's instructions before you begin, but the usual process is to use the pen to trace the pattern on the tracing paper, then place the tracing paper on the fabric and use the iron to transfer the pattern onto the fabric.
* Start by sewing the dark red areas with satin stitch.
* Stem-stitch around the reindeer with gray yarn.
* Sew the three hearts with satin stitch in blue, green, and light red.

(Continued on page 26.)

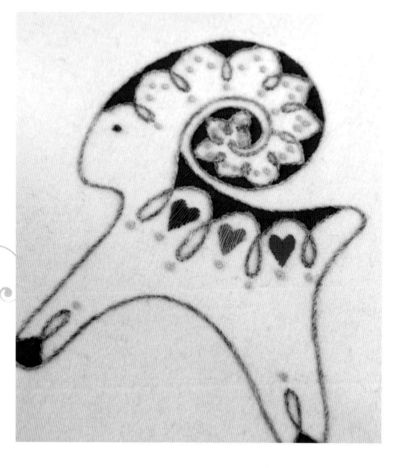

* Finish with French knots, one for the eye of the reindeer, and the rest as decorative yellow knots. Follow the pictures for guidance.
* Place the work between damp fabric pieces.

The pom-poms in the corners are made from cotton fabrics that are cut diagonally with a rotary cutter. A good size is 6 in. (15 cm) long and ½ in. (1.3 cm) wide. You need about 30 pieces for each corner, meaning you would need to cut 120 ribbons in total.

* Place the front and back pieces, right side to right side, and pin the pieces together. Place the pom-pom ribbons in each corner like you can see in the picture. The corner should be sewn with a diagonal seam. Place pins to mark the width of the pom-poms; you can also draw the seam on each corner beforehand.
* Sew the pillow pieces together, but leave an opening about 4 in. (10 cm) long. Stuff the pillow, then stitch up the opening with small stitches. Cut the ribbons diagonally. It looks best if they are not cut in the exact same length.

POM-POMS

You can of course decorate the corners as you wish; I chose to make ribbons in matching fabrics. To keep them from fraying, I've cut them diagonally with a rotary cutter. It is best to stuff the pillow with carded wool for the right weight and feeling. You can also use polyester fiberfill.

Here is another piece of wool embroidery that you can enjoy for many years to come. You can use it as a Christmas tree skirt or even as a tablecloth. It may not be suitable for the dining table, since it is made out of wool, but when used on a side table it could be a nice eye-catcher in the living room.

Materials

* Pattern and tracing paper
* Gray and red wool fabric
* Red and white felt
* Pearl-colored buttons
* Wool yarn (colors listed below)
* Scissors, ruler, pen
* Sewing machine
* Iron
* Sewing needle and thread
* Pins

WOOL YARN
* Yellow
* White
* Gray
* Red

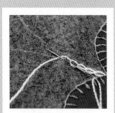

Christmas Tree Skirt or Tablecloth

In my house, we always have a table where we have nuts, oranges, marzipan, and other Christmas treats that the guests can help themselves to. It is left out throughout Christmas. (It might not be the best thing for the waistline, but it is very cozy. And at Christmas you aren't supposed to count calories, right?)

The tablecloth is embroidered with chain stitch, stem stitch, buttonhole, satin stitch, and decorative French knots. The edges are red ribbons of wadmal that are sewn on with a sewing machine.

I used wadmal, a heavy Scandinavian wool fabric, for the top and edge pieces, and a more inexpensive, lighter wool fabric for the backing. To keep the two layers together you should sew on the buttons and the white and red crosses through both layers at the very end.

DIRECTIONS:

* Cut out all the pieces: the front piece is gray wool fabric, 30 x 30 in. (76 x 76 cm); the edges are red wool, two pieces 4½ x 30 in. (11 x 76 cm) and two pieces 4½ x 35 in. (11 x 90 cm); the backing is gray wool, 39 x 39 in. (98 x 98 cm).

* Transfer the pattern drawings (big and small heart and reindeer) from page 120 and 121 to paper and cut them out. Draw and cut out four big red hearts, four white reindeer, and four small white hearts.

* Use a tape measure and chalk to make some lines to help you place the items. I've placed the hearts in the corners and the reindeer in the middle on each side. Pin the pieces to the gray front piece, and sew them on with even buttonhole stitches. Use yellow yarn for the reindeer, gray for the big hearts, and red yarn for the small hearts.

(Continued on page 31.)

✳ Sew French knots with yellow yarn around the big hearts.

✳ Embroider "antennae" from each heart with white chain stitches and finish with a red knot at the end.

✳ Place the two shorter red edges, right side to right side, on each side of the tree skirt/tablecloth. Pin and sew together. Press the seams open before you sew the last two (longer) edges.

✳ Place the tree skirt/tablecloth on top of the gray, thin wool fabric, wrong side to wrong side. Fold the excess gray fabric in half, then fold it over the top piece all around the edge and press and pin in place. Fold the corners back out and cut them diagonally to prevent them from getting too thick (a cloth corner).

✳ Sew on the whole edge by hand using small stitches.

✳ Sew through all the layers, and attach the buttons to the small hearts and to each corner between the red edge and the gray front piece. To finish, sew three white crosses between the edge and the front piece on each of the sides, and three red crosses in the middle of each reindeer.

Christmas Décor

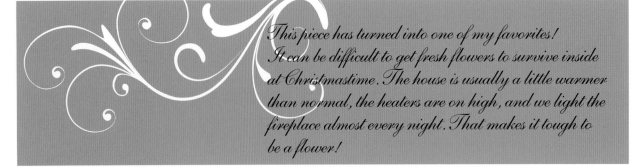

This piece has turned into one of my favorites! It can be difficult to get fresh flowers to survive inside at Christmastime. The house is usually a little warmer than normal, the heaters are on high, and we light the fireplace almost every night. That makes it tough to be a flower!

Materials

* Pattern and tracing paper
* White linen
* Large white beads
* Strong thread
* Long sewing needle
* Fiberfill
* Scissors
* Pins
* Chalk
* Pen
* Branch
* Zinc pot
* Hobby clay
* Nice rocks

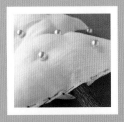

Soft Christmas Tree in a Pot

With soft Christmas trees like these, your window frame doesn't have to be empty after all. You can easily make your own variations by using colored beads and colored pots.

I've chosen this light-colored option with white linen and large, classic white beads. To contrast the delicate and soft, I've used a coarse branch to even it out, along with natural rocks and a zinc pot. You will need something heavy in the pot to make the tree stand up straight. The easiest thing is to use some hobby clay; you can stick the branch into the clay before covering it in rocks. You can also fill the whole pot with rocks and just stick the branch in between them. That will give the pot enough weight and support, while at the same time making it decorative.

On page 54 you can find a few more (and easier to make) Christmas trees.

DIRECTIONS:

* Transfer the pattern to the white linen. You will need two pieces.
* Place the trees, right side to right side, and sew them together. Leave an opening down by the "trunk."
* Cut down the seam allowance and cut the corners diagonally, then reverse the tree.
* Stuff the tree firmly with fiberfill.
* Sew on beads for the branch tips and on both sides. Pull a little extra to add some curves to the tree.
* Stick the branch into the tree opening and stitch it up. You have to sew all the way up to the "trunk" so it will sit tightly.
* Fill the pot with clay (or just rocks) and place the tree so it stands straight and sturdy. Fill up with nice rocks to cover the clay.

These felt ornaments are really fun to make, and really quick, so you can easily make enough to decorate your entire tree.

Materials

* Pattern or drinking glass and chalk
* Wadmal or felt (or fleece)
* Beads, sequins, buttons, etc.
* Fine yarn or perle cotton
* Ribbon (for loop)
* Sewing needle and thread
* Scissors and pen

Felt Ornaments

Decorate these ornaments with beads, buttons, and sequins— there are plenty of nice decorating materials available in crafting supply stores. Your ornaments don't have to look alike, so see this as an opportunity to use leftover buttons and beads. With some fiberfill inside, the ornaments are so soft you can't help but to squeeze them.

I'm sorry if I keep repeating myself, but in this project it is again best to use felt or a felted fabric that doesn't fray. If you want more colorful ornaments, fleece is a good alternative, and you can get it in many different colors. Finish decorating the pieces before sewing them together with decorative buttonhole stitches, while at the same time attaching a ribbon as a loop.

DIRECTIONS:

* Transfer the pattern from page 118, or use a glass and draw around it with chalk. For one ornament you will need two circular pieces in wadmal or felt.
* Sew a button to the middle of one piece.
* Continue attaching decorative items like beads and sequins. The pictures should provide some inspiration.
* Pin the circles together, wrong side to wrong side.
* Cut a piece (about 2 in. [5 cm]) from a matching ribbon or string to use as a loop, and pin it between the two pieces.
* Sew the ornament together with buttonhole stitches all the way around the edge. You attach the loop at the same time (see picture). When you are almost at the end, stuff it with as much fiberfill as you want.
* Sew the last part and secure the thread.

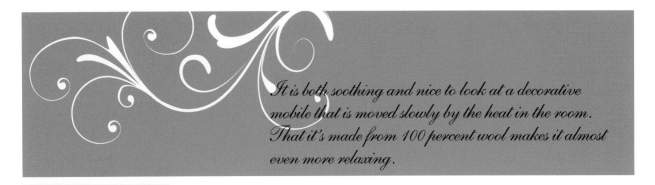

It is both soothing and nice to look at a decorative mobile that is moved slowly by the heat in the room. That it's made from 100 percent wool makes it almost even more relaxing.

Materials

* Pattern and tracing paper
* Pen
* Disappearing-ink fabric marker or chalk
* Red felt
* Red wool roving
* Soap and warm water
* A deep dish or bowl
* Red strong thread
* Long, sturdy sewing needle
* Bell (big)
* 2 dowels
* Red acrylic paint
* Paintbrush
* Scissors
* String for hanging

Red Mobile with Hearts and Balls

An extra-large bell provides a nice detail in the middle of this mobile. You can hang the mobile in a doorway, a window, or in the middle of the room—anywhere as long as it's visible!

The hearts are cut out from a sheet of red felt. The balls are felted by hand from a nice-quality wool roving. It is really fun felting wool balls and it is an activity suitable for all ages and the entire family. The stand for the mobile is made from two dowels that are painted red, and the mobile is hung from a nice "candy cane" string in red and white. Merry Christmas!

DIRECTIONS:

* Transfer the heart pattern from page 119 to a thick paper that you can use as a template.
* Draw around the template on the red felt using either a disappearing-ink fabric marker or chalk, and cut out your desired amount of hearts. Put them aside for now.
* Felted wool balls: Pour about ½ tablespoon of soap into a bowl with 1 quart of lukewarm or warm water.
* Pull out some wool and shape it into a ball. Dip the ball in the soapy water and roll it between the palms of your hands. Continue rolling and dipping it in the soapy water until the wool starts to felt.
* If the water gets cold, just make a new mix. The ratio of water to soap is not very important. When the ball is finished, squeeze it a little extra to get out as much water as possible. Leave it to dry.
* Cut the dowels to the desired length; about 12 to 14 in. (30 to 35 cm) should be good.

(Continued on page 41.)

* Paint the sticks in your chosen color and leave them to dry. Put the sticks together to make a cross and secure by winding a string around the cross. Tie together firmly, leaving the ends about 12 to 16 in. (30 to 40 cm) in length to hang the mobile.
* Cut five long pieces of the strong, red thread, and thread one into the needle. Thread it through the felt hearts and the carded balls. If the hearts and the balls don't stay in place, tie a knot underneath each decoration. To keep the mobile in balance, there should be about the same number of decorations on each of the four outer threads. Tie the big bell to the bottom of the middle thread. On my mobile this thread is the longest one.
* Tie the five decorated threads to the flower sticks, and hang the mobile.

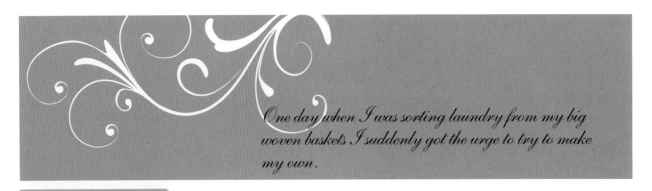

One day when I was sorting laundry from my big woven baskets I suddenly got the urge to try to make my own.

Materials

* Paper
* Craft knife
* Cutting board
* Metal ruler
* Pen
* Paper clip or clothespins
* Glue
* Scissors
* Stapler

Classic Baskets

I started making my own basket, in a smaller scale, of course, and in a completely different material that was easily accessible: normal white paper. I thought it was really fun, and it turned out to be so much easier than it looks. I would almost say I got "hooked" on making baskets, so now I have a little supply in different sizes. This basket is a perfect hostess gift; I just fill one with nice napkins and candles, or a homemade cake or cookies. It is always greatly appreciated—even outside the holiday season!

Use A4-size paper for the small basket and A3 size for the larger basket. It is better to use paper that is a little thicker than normal paper. You can use cheap paper while practicing the techniques. Look closely at the pictures of the different

steps, as they may be more effective than words. When you get started and have the paper in front of you, the steps are self-explanatory.

WEAVING THE SMALL BASKET:

* Cut 12 strips, about ½ in. (1.3 cm) wide, using the full length of an A4 sheet. Adjust the amount of strips to the size of the basket you want to make. Mark the middle of the strips and weave them together as is done in the top picture.
* Continue weaving all the strips together. Glue the edges so they stay in place.
* Draw a square diagonally across the weaving (use a ruler for help). Fold the strips up along the sides of the square.

(Continued on page 45.)

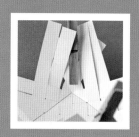

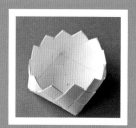

* Place the middle strips over each other in a cross and start weaving the closest strips. Secure with a paper clip or clothespin while working.

* When you get to the end of each strip, fold the edge over to the inside and glue.

WEAVING THE BIG BASKET:

* Cut 13 strips, about ½ in. (1.3 cm) wide, using the full length of the A3 sheet. Adjust the amount of strips to the size of basket you want to make. The thirteenth strip is used as an edge and a handle on this basket.

* You weave the big basket exactly like you did the small one, except for making higher edges.

* When you finish the strips, staple them so they stay in place. Cut off any excess paper.

* Cut the last strip so that it fits as an edge around the top of the basket, with a little extra for a handle. Begin by stapling the handle onto the basket. Then finish by gluing the last strip around the edge to hide all the staples.

There is nothing that says a wreath needs to be made out of a certain material. These soft fabric wreaths are just as welcoming on your door as a more traditional one.

Materials

* Pattern and tracing paper
* Chalk
* Pen and scissors
* Leftover fabrics
* Fabric for back piece
* Ribbons
* Fiberfill
* String for hanging
* Sewing machine
* Thread and pins

Soft Wreaths

The red wreath on page 49, with its fancy, patterned fabrics and ribbon with Christmas words, can hang throughout the holiday season. The beige one is meant for people who don't like red as much and would rather have the same wreath hanging throughout the year. I have decorated it with a few homemade tassels.

This is a project where you can make use of all the leftover fabrics and ribbon I am sure you have laying around—at least I know I have plenty! I collect everything and have trouble throwing anything away. Most of it I get to use at one point or another in some kind of project.

The wreaths are easily made and you can sew one in a night. I wanted to give my wreath a

"rough" look and therefore the front and back are just zigzagged together. If you want a smoother look you can always sew on the wrong side; just remember to add seam allowance if you choose this option.

DIRECTIONS:

* Transfer the pattern from page 118 to the tracing paper and draw 12 pieces. (The red wreath requires 14 pieces.)
* Pin and sew together the pieces of the front to form a wreath. Press the seam allowance.
* Place the front and back pieces, wrong side to wrong side.

(Continued on page 48.)

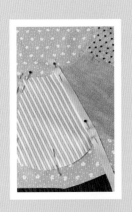

✳ Pin the pieces together. Attach ribbons between a few of the front pieces if desired.

✳ Sew the pieces together with a zigzag using a sewing machine; leave an opening of about 2 in. (5 cm) on the inside of the wreath.

✳ Cut around the seam on the outside of the wreath and stuff well with fiberfill.

✳ Stitch up the opening with a zigzag and cut around the seam in the middle.

✳ Hang the wreath with a nice string or ribbon in a suitable color, and decorate with a few tassels if desired (see page 60).

Here you can see the Christmas wreath in red fabrics and ribbon with Christmas words. The steps are the same as with the beige wreath, only this version is made with 14 pieces instead of 12.

A lovely pot for nuts or Christmas candy is made quickly and easily with a terra-cotta pot and bowl.

Materials

* Terra-cotta pot with bowl
* Water-based craft paint
* Paintbrush
* Sandpaper
* A motif, for example from a napkin
* Decoupage glue or paint
* Foam brush
* Scissors

Pot Decorated in Decoupage

This project uses the same technique (decoupage) as the cans on page 74, but it's made in a totally different style. This is probably what most would think of as decoupage. Here we decorate a regular terra-cotta pot and its bowl. The result is a pretty and practical pot on which the bowl will work as a lid. If you want to give it away as a present, tie a nice ribbon around it so the lid will stay in place.

I have used sandpaper to rub over the paint to give it more of a patina. The angel motif is from a napkin, but you can also use motifs found in wrapping paper, wallpaper, or magazines. It's just trial and error.

DIRECTIONS:

* Clean the pot properly, then paint it with craft paint in whatever color you wish.
* Use the sandpaper to rub off some of the paint here and there to make it look worn. Make sure to rub it the most at places that are most likely to be worn, like along the edges. Then brush off the pot to make sure there isn't any dust adhering to it.
* Cut out the motif you want.
* Apply a thin layer of decoupage glue or paint using a wide foam brush.
* Let the glue dry before you put on another layer or two; apply the glue or the paint all over the pot and lid.
* The pot is ready for use. Fill it up with Christmas nuts or something else delicious.

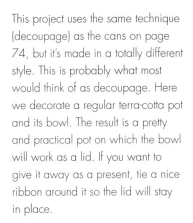

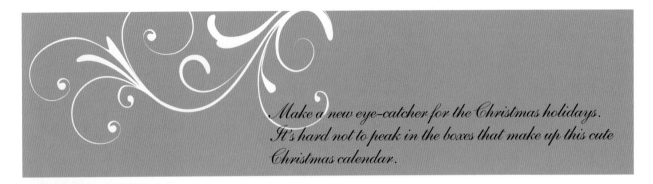

Make a new eye-catcher for the Christmas holidays. It's hard not to peak in the boxes that make up this cute Christmas calendar.

Materials

* 24 matchboxes
* Craft glue
* Template for the heart
* Pencil
* Red craft paint
* Paintbrush
* Gold pen
* Woven ribbon
* Scissors
* Strong cardboard, approximately 1 mm thick
* Red-and-white-striped cotton fabric
* Extra-strong adhesive
* Craft knife, cutting mat, metal ruler

Fun Calendar Chest of Drawers

Fill up the drawers with whatever you wish, but as you can see large items won't fit. However, there is more than enough room for well-chosen words—because it doesn't have to be chocolate or magnificent presents in a Christmas calendar. Why not tone down the holiday hysteria and write something nice and personal each day until Christmas?

I used 24 regular small matchboxes, but you can of course use large ones too. It depends on what you plan to fill the drawers with. The measurements given here for the back piece and the sides of the chest are adjusted to the standard size of a matchbox. You should measure again before you cut the fabric to make sure it matches the boxes you use. A small ribbon makes the drawers easy to open and close. Write the numbers 1 to 24 with a gold pen, and decide what motif you want on the chest. I painted a heart on this piece.

DIRECTIONS:

* Start by gluing together all the matchboxes. The easiest method is to glue together three rows with eight boxes on top of each other. Let the glue dry, and then glue the three rows together. Make sure the glue is completely dry before you continue.
* Make a heart template, place it on top of the boxes, and trace the heart.
* Paint the heart with water-based craft paint in Christmas red. Use two coats if necessary. Let it dry.
* Write simple numbers on each of the drawers; it will look great if you use a gold pen.
* Cut the ribbon into pieces about 2½ in. (6 cm) long, then fold under the end of each by ½ in. (1.3 cm) and glue. Press and hold until the glue is dry.
* Glue the single part of the ribbon under the boxes, so as to not make it too thick when you close the drawers. Let it dry.

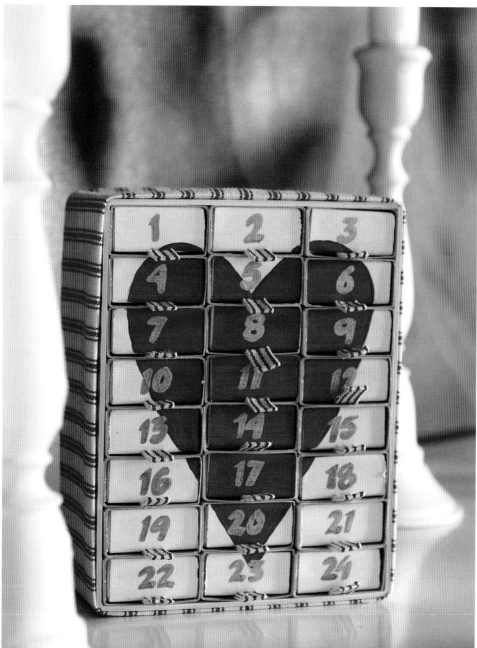

* Cut a piece of strong cardboard the same size as the back piece of the chest (in this case 4¼ x 5½ in. [10.8 x 14 cm]). Pull out the drawers, apply glue to the back of the chest, and attach the cardboard.

* Cover the sides. Cut a long piece of cardboard (here 20 x 2½ in. [50.7 x 6 cm]). Mark the cardboard to divide it into 4 segments for the sides—4½, 5½, 4½, and 5½ in. (11.1, 14.2, 11.2,

and 14.2 cm)—then score a line at each mark (where the cardboard will be folded). Glue the cardboard around the entire chest using an extra-strong glue stick. Let it dry.

* Cut a strip of fabric 21 x 5 in. (53 x 13 cm). Fold in the long sides to meet in the middle and press. Apply glue to every edge of the chest, and glue the fabric strip to it, placing the ends at the bottom.

These small and cute spruce trees only have one function—decoration! At Christmas you're allowed to indulge and decorate just for the fun of it.

Materials

* Pattern and tracing paper
* Fabric
* Fiberfill
* Pen
* Tailor's chalk
* Scissors
* Sewing machine
* Pins
* Sewing needle and sewing thread
* Perle cotton

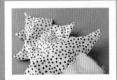

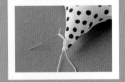

Soft Christmas Trees

These sewn trees are fun to make; you might as well make several while you're at it. You may vary the choice of fabric and the sizes of the trees. The only things you need are a piece of fabric and some fiberfill and you are on your way to sewing your own spruce forest. These trees are also perfect for giving as small, homemade gifts.

It is easiest to use thin cotton fabrics. Check your leftover box before buying new fabrics, as there is most likely something in there you can use! When the trees are finished, hang them on an available peg rail in the hallway, or place them in between pillows on the couch. They are decorative wherever they are!

DIRECTIONS:

* Transfer the pattern from the pattern sheet to the tracing paper and cut it out.
* Fold the fabric at the middle, right side to right side, and pin the layers together.
* Draw the spruce pattern using tailor's chalk.
* Sew around the chalk line, but leave an opening of approximately 2½ in. (5 cm) at the bottom of the tree.
* Cut out the tree with as little seam allowance as possible.
* Fill the spruce with fiberfill; make sure every corner is filled.
* Pin the opening together and close it with small stitches sewn by hand.
* Sew a small loop of perle cotton to the top of the tree if you plan to hang it.

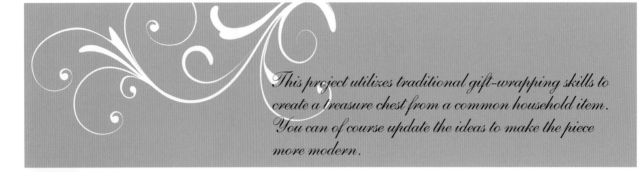

This project utilizes traditional gift-wrapping skills to create a treasure chest from a common household item. You can of course update the ideas to make the piece more modern.

Materials

* 4 boxes of matches
* Strong cardboard
* Fabric
* Craft knife
* Cutting mat
* Metal ruler
* Glue
* Ribbon

Pretty Matchboxes

Decorating a box of matches is an old classic we've almost forgotten about. By keeping this "four-sided" box on the table you will always have matches when you need them, without searching your whole house looking for them!

You can use matchboxes of any size; the method remains the same. Cover strong cardboard with pretty fabrics, and glue the fabric-covered cardboard onto the boxes of matches. Attach small ribbons as handles to make it easy to open the boxes.

DIRECTIONS:

* Place the matchboxes in the formation you want, on top of a piece of strong cardboard. Draw the outline, but add ⅒ in. (3 mm) around each side. Cut out two identical pieces of cardboard.
* Place the cardboard on the fabric and cut with about ¾ in. (2 cm)

allowance around the cardboard. Oblique-cut the corners, and then apply glue to the wrong side of the allowance and in the corners. Glue the fabric to the cardboard.

* Cut the ribbon into four pieces about 2½ in. (6 cm) long, then fold under the end of each by ½ in. (1.3 cm) and glue. Press the fold until the glue is dry. These will be the handles used to open the "drawers."
* Glue the single short side of the ribbon inside the box so that it will not be too thick when you close the "drawers." Let the glue dry.
* Glue all four boxes of matches onto one of the pieces of cardboard with fabric. Apply glue to the matchboxes and attach the other piece of cardboard with fabric by pressing.
* Insert the matchboxes—you are ready to light all the Christmas candles!

Materials

* Boxes of matches
* Pattern and tracing paper (for the box decorated in beads)
* Sewing needle and thread (for the box decorated in beads)
* Small red beads, sequins, or buttons
* Fabric
* Japanese paper (washi)
* Strong cardboard
* Cutting mat
* Craft knife
* Metal ruler
* Glue
* Scissors
* Pen
* Disappearing-ink fabric marker

Matchboxes with Beads, Sequins, and Buttons

These decorated matchboxes are a bit simpler than the previous project, and I've used larger boxes, so one or two per project is enough. The mood will soon be more festive when you use sparkling beads, sequins, or nice buttons. You don't need much more to decorate the boxes.

The boxes are covered with linen fabric or Japanese paper. For the large box you can sew small red beads onto the white linen. On the other two boxes you may glue sequins and a nice white button directly onto the white Japanese paper surface. One box is double and the other is a single box. The linen fabric and Japanese paper are first glued to strong cardboard before you place the boxes together. You do not need to mount handles because you can push from the back side of the box.

DIRECTIONS:

* Place the matchboxes on top of a piece of strong cardboard. Draw the outline, but add ⅛ in. (2 mm) around each side. Cut out two identical cardboard pieces.
* Place the cardboard on the fabric or Japanese paper and cut out, adding an allowance of about 1 in. (2.5 cm) all the way around.
* Transfer the heart pattern from page 118 to the linen fabric, preferably using a disappearing-ink fabric marker. Sew red beads along the outline of the heart, and attach the thread on the wrong side.
* Place the fabric or Japanese paper onto the cardboard, oblique-cut the corners, and apply glue to the wrong side of the allowance and corners. Attach to the cardboard with glue.
* Glue the decorations to the Japanese paper version.

58

A decorative tassel can be used anywhere. Attach it to a knob on a cabinet door or drawer, or use tassels at the end of a Christmas tablecloth or as decoration on a wreath or an Advent calendar.

Materials

* Felt
* Scissors
* Ruler
* Glue
* Tailor's chalk

Decorative Felt Tassels

You will find these felt tassels used in various projects in this book (the stocking calendar on page 20, the bright fabric wreath on page 46, and napkin ring on page 68), but I'm sure you have tons of other ideas on where to place them. Your own imagination is the limit.

Make the tassels in felt or a felted fabric that doesn't fray. There is no seam; you only cut and use glue. So the tassels don't require too much time to make!

DIRECTIONS:

* Cut one 4 x 8 in. (10 x 20 cm) piece of felt and another strip that is ½ x 6 in. (1.3 x 15 cm).
* Cut notches about 2¾ in. (7 cm) deep in the long side of the larger piece of felt. Space the cuts about ¼ in. (0.6 cm) apart.
* Apply glue to the end of the other strip of felt and press together to make a loop.
* Apply some glue to one of the ends of the tassel. Glue the loop to the tassel.
* Apply a generous amount of glue to the uncut part of the tassel.
* Roll the tassel together tight, and hold it together until the glue has set.

Christmas Table Decorations

This decoration is not only for Christmas—I think it suits any occasion. It might fit particularly well at a New Year's party, where decorations are allowed to sparkle a bit more than usual. A New Year's wedding would be the ultimate occasion for this decoration.

Materials

* Papier mâché hearts
* White craft paint
* Water-based paint
* Gold leaf and silver leaf
* Craft adhesive
* Ribbon
* Color wash brush
* Paintbrush
* Soft brush

Glamorous Heart Favors

It's exciting to work with gold and silver leaf. You can find all the materials needed for this project in a crafting supply store or wherever they sell art supplies. There are different price ranges, from regular "craft prices" to very expensive.

The heart of papier mâché can be bought at a craft supply store. You can get all kinds of shapes and sizes, but hearts and stars are the easiest to find—and both are well suited for Christmas. Let the favors, decorated with gold and silver, dominate the table, and use a nice white tablecloth, white napkins, and simple classic glasses. You will make a glamorous impression through the decorations, which will sparkle and welcome your guests.

DIRECTIONS:

* Paint the heart completely white. Use several layers if necessary. Let it dry.
* Dip the color wash brush in paint and make a circle imprint on the heart.
* Carefully apply a piece of gold or silver leaf. Push with a soft brush and an easy hand over the metal. Let it dry before you continue with more circles.
* Brush off excess gold or silver leaf using the soft brush.
* When you have made as many gold and silver circles as you want, paint the whole heart with the water-based paint and then let it dry.
* Glue small decorative glass stones (that are flat in the back) in the middle of each circle. Finish by tying a pretty ribbon in the loop on top.

Set an elegant Christmas table. Handmade napkin rings made of wool balls and matching glass beads— that's stylish!

Materials

* Elastic thread
* Wool for felting
* Soap
* Lukewarm or hot water
* Beads
* Sewing needle

Napkin Ring with Wool Balls

If you thread the balls and beads on an elastic thread (jewelry thread), the napkin ring can also be used as a bracelet. Why not let your female guests take their napkin ring home as an extra Christmas gift from the host?

You can use different types of wool to felt the balls. Carded lamb's wool, Nepal wool, or merino wool; all these are well suited. When the wool balls and beads are threaded on an elastic thread, it's easier to thread the napkin ring around the napkin. There are wool balls—with beads in between—only on the upper side of the ring. On the bottom it is only glass beads. Both beads and wool exist in numerous colors, so you can easily pick the color you like the most and that goes with the rest of your table. I think this deep red is perfect for Christmas.

DIRECTIONS:

* Felted wool balls: Pour approximately ½ tablespoon of soap in a bowl with 1 quart (1 liter) of lukewarm or hot water.

* Pull out some wool and shape it into a ball. Dip the ball into the soapy water and roll it between your palms. Continue to roll and dip until the wool felts up.

* If the water turns cold, make a new mix with warm water. The exact ratio of soap to water is not too important. When the ball is done, squeeze it extra hard between your palms to remove as much water as possible. Let the balls dry. When the balls are dry, cut a piece of the elastic thread and thread it on a sewing needle that will fit through the beads.

* Thread on the beads and wool balls. I used five wool balls with one bead between each, and enough beads on the bottom to shape a ring. The number of beads depends on how large you want to make the rings, and how large your beads (and wool balls) are. I used about 16 beads for the bottom.

* Finish by tying the ends together in a firm knot—simple and easy.

Materials

* Felt or wool fabric that doesn't fray
* Scissors
* Ruler
* Glue
* Tailor's chalk
* Beads
* Strong sewing thread
* Sewing needle
* Ribbon

Pearl-Decorated Napkin Ring

Follow the instructions for the felt tassel on page 60, but make a short loop and add a few beads. You will then have a stylish and elegant napkin ring for you and your guests. Choose beads that match the tassel. This will leave an overall nice impression. If you are making napkin rings for a big party, you can of course settle for the tassels only, as sewing on beads is pretty time consuming. You don't have to sew beads all the way around; a little over halfway is enough, since that's the only part showing.

DIRECTIONS:

* Make the tassel as described on page 60, but make the loop shorter. The finished loop should be approximately ¾ in. (2 cm) long.
* Sew beads close together on the part of the tassel that will be visible.
* Thread a ribbon through the short loop. Leave long ends that you can tie under the napkin, or sew the ribbon together by hand with a few stitches. Hide the splice inside the tassel loop.

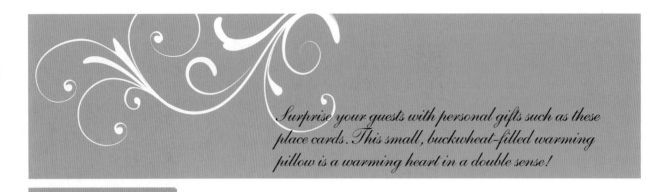

Materials

* Pattern and tracing paper
* Pen
* Scissors
* Disappearing-ink fabric marker
* Tailor's chalk
* Fabric
* Red ribbon or red string
* Perle cotton
* Sewing needle
* Pins
* Whole buckwheat or rice
* Funnel

A Warm Heart Place Card

Embroider the guest's name on the heart and fill it with either rice or buckwheat. The finished pillow will maintain a comfortable heat after spending a few minutes in the microwave. It can sooth a tired and aching body after a long day on the slopes or a stressful day at work! I promise you this generous gesture will be a success among your friends.

I've chosen natural-colored linen because I feel it's suitable for both winter and summer. You can change the table accessories to match the season—red for Christmas, or something like white for summer. If you have a natural-colored linen tablecloth in your closet, that's basically all you need!

It's best to use a sturdy fabric for these hearts, like linen or cotton. Write in your own handwriting, or use the computer for help. Embroider the name or another motif using perle cotton.

DIRECTIONS:

* Transfer the pattern from page 116 to tracing paper, and cut it out.
* Place the heart template on the fabric, and draw the outline using tailor's chalk.
* Write your guest's name or draw another motif using the disappearing-ink fabric marker; embroider the outline stitches with perle cotton.
* Place the embroidered heart with the right side down on the fabric you are using as a back piece, and pin the two pieces together. Place the ribbon or string you are using for the loop in between the layers.
* Sew the seam around the heart, but leave a small opening.
* Cut out the heart with as little seam allowance as possible and turn it right side out.
* Fill the heart with either whole buckwheat or rice.
* Pin together and close the opening with small stitches you can sew by hand.

It's always a pleasure being a guest where the hosts have really made an effort with the table decorations. Here, each guest will get their own little Christmas tree with their name on it.

Materials

*   Pattern and tracing paper
*   Paper for the trees
*   Pen
*   Scissors
*   Sewing machine
*   Sewing thread
*   Gold paper for the star
*   Gold pen

Christmas Tree Place Cards

This project might look advanced and time consuming, but it is actually not. It is very easy to cut and sew together the place card trees, because they are in fact sewn together on a machine. I've decorated the trees with simple small dots in gold, and on top I've placed a sparkling gold star. Write the guest's name with a gold pen, and place each tree on a small, round doily cake napkin.

Personally I think white is nicest, but you are of course free to experiment and make trees in whatever colors you like. Use a firm paper, a little thicker than regular copy paper, but not so thick that you can't sew through two layers with the sewing machine.

DIRECTIONS:

*   Transfer the pattern from page 118 to tracing paper you can use as a template.
*   Trace the pattern on your choice of paper, and then cut it out. You need two parts for each tree.
*   Trace the pattern and cut out the stars, one for each tree.
*   Place the two parts of the tree on top of each other, and sew them together with straight stitches using the sewing machine. Start about ½ in. (1.3 cm) from the top to ensure there is room for the star.
*   Fold out the tree and make it stand.
*   Draw small dots in gold, and finish by writing the name of the guest on one of the branches near the bottom.
*   Put the star on top of the tree, and place it on a doily cake napkin with a lace edge.

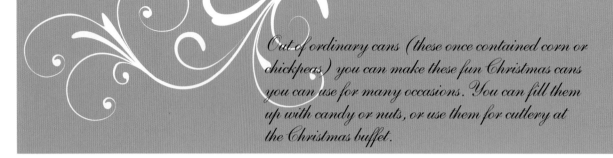

Out of ordinary cans (these once contained corn or chickpeas) you can make these fun Christmas cans you can use for many occasions. You can fill them up with candy or nuts, or use them for cutlery at the Christmas buffet.

Materials

* Cans
* Napkin or other motif
* White craft paint
* Paintbrush
* Decoupage glue or paint
* Foam brush
* String
* Glue
* Scissors

Nice Decoupage Cans

The cans are decorated with nice motifs taken from Christmas napkins, and they're both fun and easy to make. Fill a can with homemade Christmas candy and give it away as a Christmas present—it will be a success!

It is important that the cans are completely clean before you paint them with a base of white paint. When the paint is dry, find the motif you want to use, and go to work with scissors and glue. You can buy napkins with all kinds of motifs. Do what I do: Whenever I travel I always buy napkins to bring home with me. Some I use for their intended purpose as napkins but most end up in my craft drawer.

DIRECTIONS:

* Clean the can properly and let it dry.
* Paint the can with white craft paint. Make sure the can is completely covered. Use several coats if necessary.
* Cut the napkin so it fits the can.
* With a foam brush, apply a layer of decoupage glue or paint over the whole can, and carefully place the napkin on top. Smooth out the napkin using the foam brush.
* When the surface is dry, apply another layer of decoupage glue or paint, covering the whole can. Let it dry.
* Glue a string around the opening of the can to make it look complete.

Christmas Greetings

*These are my favorites among my Christmas cards.
They are fun to make and a pleasure to receive.
They are a bit time consuming, but you don't have to
make these for all of your relatives—maybe just for
your closest friends.*

Materials

* Pattern for the spruce tree
* Blue and green thin cardboard (A4)
* Patterned paper
* Glue stick
* White paper
* Toothpick to roll paper around
* Gold star
* Glue
* White Japanese paper (washi)
* Beads or small decorative gems with one flat side
* Scissors
* Craft knife
* Cutting mat
* Metal ruler

Imaginative Snow Cards

You can make your own version of this card using any beautiful paper and decorative materials you have available. You can mix all kinds of materials. The "snowflakes" are tightly rolled strips of paper. Paper that is meant for scrapbooking is perfect for these cards. The snow is ripped white Japanese paper. As you can see, you can use almost anything. This is a project to which the whole family can contribute.

DIRECTIONS:

* Fold the two cardboards at the middle. Here I've used an A4 format, but choose the size you want.
* Cut the patterned paper with scissors or craft knife so it ends up being ½ in. (1.3 cm) smaller than the card (on all four sides). Glue it to the front of the card with a glue stick. All glued papers have a tendency to curl,

so leave the cards pressed for a while so they will be nice and smooth.

* Trace the spruce tree pattern on page 118 onto a patterned paper and cut it out. Glue the tree to the blue card.
* Tear one side of the Japanese paper so it makes a "snow border." Glue the Japanese paper to the bottom of the card to represent snow. For the green card without the spruce tree, I've glued the Japanese paper diagonally over the front, resembling a snow-covered hill.
* Glue the gold star on top of the tree and onto the sky.
* Cut strips of the white paper about ¼ in. (0.6 cm) wide. Roll the paper around the toothpick and glue the end to the card to create a "snowflake."
* Glue the snowflakes and beads to the cards.

A Christmas present doesn't have to be very big to be appreciated. A small envelope with large content is probably just as welcome! For the person who has everything, a gift card is the solution. And the gift card can be anything; a day at the spa will probably be a very popular gift!

Envelope and Bookmark in Silver and Gray

Materials

* Paper or thin cardboard in gray tones
* Silver metallic paper
* Black-and-white angel pictures
* Metal ruler
* Cutting mat
* Craft knife
* Hole puncher
* Pen
* Double-sided adhesive tape
* Relief liner
* White satin ribbon
* Mother-of-pearl beads or other embellishments
* Glue

Depending on how large you make the envelope, it could have room for more than just a flat gift card; I'm sure a CD (or a diamond ring!) can fit! It's wise to use paper meant for scrapbooking, as these papers have just the right thickness and they come in a number of colors and patterns. Decorate the envelopes as you wish. Here are my suggestions.

DIRECTIONS:

* Measure the dimensions for the envelope. In the size I've made mine, one scrapbooking paper is enough for two envelopes (cut two pieces 5 x 12 in. [13 x 30 cm]) and one bookmark (2 x 6 in. [5 x 15 cm]). If you need room for a CD, the envelope must be 6 x 12 in. (15 x 30 cm). Cut the paper with a craft knife.
* Fold the paper at the middle, and press the fold with the back side of the craft knife to make a nice, sharp fold.
* Use a narrow, double-sided adhesive tape and attach the

envelope together along the sides. It should have an opening at the top.
* Cut the angel motifs with scissors or a craft knife. As you can see in the pictures, I have one round and one square motif. Search the Internet if you can't find any good motifs at home.
* Glue the motifs to the silver metallic paper, and cut them out. Leave about a ¼ in. (6 mm) wide frame around the motifs.
* Place the motifs on the front side of the card with double-sided adhesive tape.
* Decorate with either small dots using a mother of pearl-colored relief pen, or glue a bead in each corner of the motif. The bookmark has a slightly larger bead.
* Make two holes in the envelope using the hole puncher and put in the presents. Then thread the ribbon through the hole and make a pretty bow.

You can use these cards as regular Christmas cards; just write a nice greeting and mail them. Or you can use them as Christmas present cards and put money or gift cards together with the card inside the envelope.

Materials

* Brown and red paper or thin cardboard
* Gold metallic paper
* Christmas motif
* Gold pen
* Ribbon in brown and red
* Double-sided adhesive tape
* Double-sided adhesive tape cushions
* Red metal thread
* Metal ruler
* Craft knife
* Cutting mat
* Hole puncher
* Pen
* Scissors

Brown Antique Envelopes

Here I've taken the easy way out and bought an adhesive Christmas motif. You never get tired of that old-fashioned Santa.

It's fun to combine different types of paper. It's a good idea to start with the motif and then find colors that match it later. You'll end up with a harmonic and professional look. I think double-sided adhesive cushions are an excellent invention. They make it easy to give the card a 3-D effect.

DIRECTIONS:

* Measure and mark the envelopes. One piece of scrapbooking paper is enough for two: one large (cut a piece 8 x 12 in. [20 x 30 cm]) and one small (4 x 12 in. [10 x 30 cm]). Cut out a card in any style you choose to fit in each envelope. The small card should fit inside entirely, and the large card should be a little taller than the envelope.
* Fold the papers at the middle, and press the fold with the back side of the craft knife to make a nice, sharp fold.
* Use a narrow double-sided tape to attach the sides of the envelopes together. They must have an opening at the top for you to put in cards and/or presents.
* Place and glue the motif on the gold metallic paper, and then cut it out with about a ³⁄₁₆ in. (5 mm) gold frame. Attach the motif to the envelope with double-sided adhesive cushions. This will give it the nice 3-D effect.
* Use the hole puncher to punch a hole on top of the small envelope. Put your gift inside, thread the ribbon through, and tie a nice bow.
* Use the hole puncher to punch a hole in the card for the large envelope. If you want, write a nice Christmas note to go with the money or a gift card.
* Attach a nice ribbon through the hole in the card. Here I've tied a red metal thread around the ribbon instead of tying a bow. Put the card in the envelope.

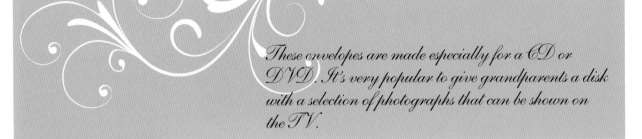

These envelopes are made especially for a CD or DVD. It's very popular to give grandparents a disk with a selection of photographs that can be shown on the TV.

Materials

* Red, striped, and natural-colored paper or thin cardboard
* Buttons
* Ribbon
* String
* Gold pen
* Thin black felt pen
* Gold-colored stamp pad
* Hole puncher
* Double-sided tape
* Metal ruler
* Cutting mat
* Craft knife or scissors
* Pen

Button-Decorated Case

It's wise to use a sturdy and thick paper for this project. Scrapbooking paper is perfect. You can buy plastic covers for the CDs if you don't want to put them straight into the case. The decorative button works as a clasp for the case.

DIRECTIONS:

* Measure and mark the size of the cases (for a standard case, cut a piece 6 x 12 in. [15 x 30 cm]). Cut out with scissors or a craft knife.
* Fold the papers at the middle, and press the fold with the back side of the craft knife to make a nice, sharp fold.
* Use a narrow double-sided tape and glue the cases together along the sides. They must have an opening at the top for you to put in CDs or DVDs.
* Cut circles or squares for name tags.
* Cut circles or squares slightly bigger than the name tags.
* Pull a gold-colored stamp pad along the sides of the name tags and the patterned paper that will be the frame around the name tag. Leave it to dry so the gold won't stain elsewhere.
* Attach the different pieces together using the double-sided tape. Write the name with a wide gold pen and, if you can, make a shadow using a black felt pen.
* Punch a hole at the top of the case, through both layers. Put a CD inside. Attach the button by threading the string or ribbon through the button and hole on the case and tying a bow at the back.

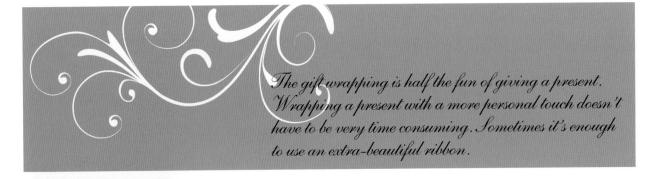

The gift wrapping is half the fun of giving a present. Wrapping a present with a more personal touch doesn't have to be very time consuming. Sometimes it's enough to use an extra-beautiful ribbon.

Materials

* Gray wrapping paper
* Wide ribbon
* Small doilies
* Gray cardboard
* Double-sided adhesive cushion
* White pen
* Glue stick
* Tape
* Scissors

Elegant Wrapping in Shades of Gray

It's always nice to have some wrapping paper around, so I usually buy some here and there when I see something nice. Gray is probably not the first color you think of when you are about to wrap your Christmas presents, but I think it can look very elegant. Even the pickiest receiver will enjoy a present like this under the tree.

DIRECTIONS:

* Wrap as you usually would; it's prettiest if you hide the tape. Fold the tape in three or use double-sided tape, and attach at the inside of the paper.
* Wrap the ribbon once around the present, and attach at the bottom.
* Glue a small doily to the middle of the present
* Cut a circle out of the gray cardboard; you can use a glass as a template.
* Write a note on the cardboard circle with the white pen and glue it to the middle of the doily. For best results, use a double-sided adhesive cushion.

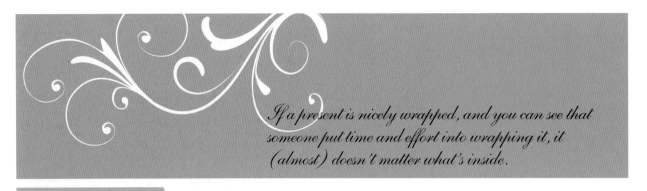

If a present is nicely wrapped, and you can see that someone put time and effort into wrapping it, it (almost) doesn't matter what's inside.

Materials

* * Gray wrapping paper
* * Tape
* * Scissors
* * Silver-colored fabric ribbon
* * Brooch
* * Prism
* * Silver thread (for the prism)

Present with Prisms and Brooches

For this project you can use old jewelry or the Christmas decorations you bought on sale last January. The delicate gray and silver tones are a pretty combination.

DIRECTIONS:

* ✻ Wrap as you usually would; it's prettiest if you hide the tape. Fold the tape in three or use double-sided tape, and attach at the inside of the paper.

* ✻ Tie the gray fabric ribbon around the presents.
* ✻ Cut the ends into beveled tips or tips to each side, starting in the middle.
* ✻ Attach a brooch over the knot at one of the presents
* ✻ . . . and attach a prism in a silver thread to the other.

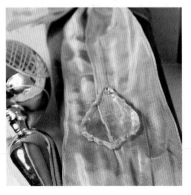

Here is a different and nice way to wrap a small Christmas present. It will be so nice the receiver won't want to open it—but it's possible to close it again!

Materials

* Pattern and tracing paper
* White, colored, or patterned paper
* Metal ruler
* Craft knife
* Cutting mat
* Pen
* Double-sided adhesive tape
* Glue
* Tape in case of splices
* Ribbon with small pom-poms
* Ribbon
* Scissors
* Hole puncher for the tag

Christmas Tree Gift Box

The ribbon has small pom-poms that make great Christmas balls, and the round tag will make sure the receiver gets the message. Here, you can say the wrapping is a gift in itself.

You need a large sheet of paper to make the Christmas tree present. If you use an A3 sheet, you can just splice the sides together. If you want another size it's easy to increase or reduce the size of the tree. Use a relatively thick and sturdy paper to make the tree strong enough to "hold" the contents. Decorate the tree the way you wish. Only your imagination can limit you. If you use a patterned paper, it's decoration enough in itself.

DIRECTIONS:

* Transfer the pattern from the tracing paper to the paper you want to use. If you need to splice the paper to make it wide enough, attach the ends with regular tape.

* Cut the Christmas tree in the paper you have chosen.
* Fold the paper along the dotted line in the pattern.
* Tape the box together using double-sided adhesive tape (see picture).
* Make a hole at the top with a hole puncher.
* Glue the pom-pom ribbon on as Christmas decorations.
* Make a round (or square) tag, and make a hole with the hole puncher.
* Put the present inside, fold the flaps, and attach the ribbon to the hole at the top of the tree. Attach the tag to the end of the ribbon and tie a knot to keep it in place.
* Don't forget to write a name on the tag—everyone is going to want this gift!

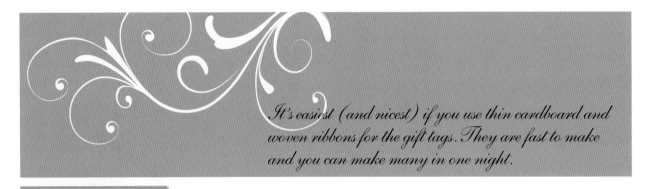

It's easiest (and nicest) if you use thin cardboard and woven ribbons for the gift tags. They are fast to make and you can make many in one night.

Materials

* Pattern
* Woven ribbons with Christmas words
* Cardboard in different colors
* Double-sided adhesive tape
* Hole puncher
* Craft knife
* Cutting mat
* Metal ruler
* String
* Glue

Gift Tags

You can find the ribbons used in this project in arts and crafts stores. Attach the ribbon over the whole gift tag or just at the top if you want to leave space for writing a name.

My examples show easy and classic-looking gift tags in red and white. But with large selections of ribbons, paper, and cardboard available at the stores, you can easily make your own versions. Think about the receiver; it's always nice to make something especially for him or her.

DIRECTIONS:

* Transfer the small tag pattern from page 121 to a piece of cardboard, and cut out.
* Cut a suitable length of the ribbon with text, and glue it to the tag.
* Attach the tag to a larger piece of cardboard in another color. You can use double-sided adhesive tape if you want to.
* Cut a few millimeters outside the tag so there will be a frame around it.
* Make a hole with the hole puncher.
* Thread a suitable string through the hole and attach the tag to the present.

Personal Christmas Gifts

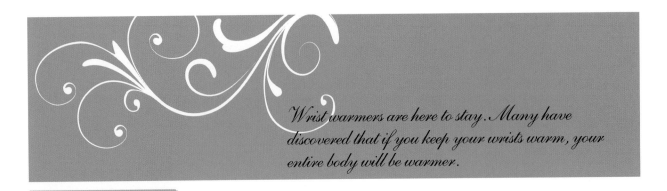

Wrist warmers are here to stay. Many have discovered that if you keep your wrists warm, your entire body will be warmer.

Wrist Warmers for Mom

Materials

* Pattern and tracing paper
* Fleece or felt
* Scissors
* Pins
* Sewing machine
* Extra-strong sewing thread
* Decorative elements
* Yarn and crochet hook (optional)

This style of wrist warmers goes back a long time, long before fleece was on the market. Back in those days people used to knit or felt them; today you can quickly and easily sew a pair that is just as good out of ready-made felt or fleece. Your personality can show through in the decoration. You can decorate them in a number of different ways, but here are some of my suggestions. It's easiest to use ready-made decorative elements, like these cute fabric roses or the white embroidered ornament. A little bit more time consuming, but still doable, are the snow crystals I made out of small beads.

I recommend using a fabric that doesn't fray. Fleece or wool felt is nice and warm to have around your wrists. These materials also come in many different colors. Add the embellishments before you sew the wrist warmers together. It's a good idea to use an elastic seam, but if you can't make one with your sewing machine, use a narrow zigzag seam instead.

For an extra-special touch, make a nice edge with a crochet border or blanket stitches along the opening.

DIRECTIONS:

* Transfer the pattern to tracing paper, and cut out. Cut out all four parts together for one pair of wrist warmers.
* Decorate as you wish.
* Pin the pieces together, right side to right side, and sew together with an elastic seam.
* Turn the wrist warmers inside out so the right side is out. If you want a crochet border or a border of blanket stitches, do it now, after the wrist warmers are sewn together.
* Crochet border: Pick up single crochet stitches along the edge and crochet the round with single crochet stitches.

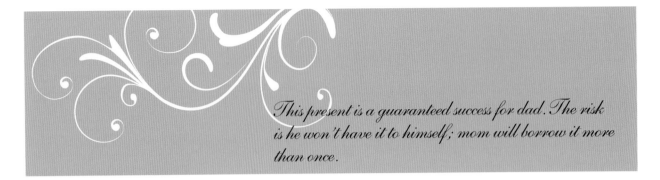

This present is a guaranteed success for dad. The risk is he won't have it to himself; mom will borrow it more than once.

Materials

* Wool fabric of good quality
* Wool yarn for blanket stitches and tassels
* Needle
* Scissors
* A piece of cardboard for the tassels

A Nice Warm Scarf for Dad

The wool fabric used for this scarf is very soft and comfortable. The blanket stitches are sewn out of wool scrap yarn. It is good to vary the colors on the seam and make little matching tassels around the scarf.

Make the scarf as large as you want. A large one is appreciated in colder areas. The blanket stitches are easy to make, and little tassels can be attached in the transitions between the different colors. This way the splices won't be visible, and the scarf will look the same on each side.

DIRECTIONS:

* Cut the scarf to a desired size. This one is 12 x 60 in. (30 x 152 cm).
* Use wool scrap yarn and sew blanket stitches in different colors around the whole scarf.
* When you come to the end of a piece of yarn, leave a loose end that you can tie the tassel to later. See picture.
* Continue sewing with the new color, and make all the tassels at the end.
* To make the tassel, wrap the yarn about eight times around a piece of cardboard about 2 in. (5 cm) wide.
* Use the loose threads on the scarf to wrap and tie on the tassel.
* Cut the loops at the other end of the tassel.

You don't have to be a kid to fall in love with these colorful crocheted balls. They are also very decorative in a bowl on the coffee table! Crochet them in a single color or make them striped, like the ones shown here.

Materials

* Yarn in different colors
* Crochet hook that fits the yarn
* Scissors
* Fiberfill
* Needle with a blunt tip

Crocheted Toy Balls

You can use any kind of yarn: cotton, acrylic, or wool. If you are making striped balls, make sure to pick yarns of the same thickness.

DIRECTIONS:

* Ch 5. Join with a sl st to form a ring.
* **Round 1:** Ch 1, work 10 sc in the ring, join with a sl st in beg ch.
* **Round 2:** Ch 1, *sc in next 2 sts, 2 sc in next st, rep from * around, join with a sl st in beg ch.
* **Round 3:** Ch 1, *sc in next 3 sts, 2 sc in next st, rep from * around, join with a sl st in beg ch.
* **Round 4:** Ch 1, *sc in next 4 sts, 2 sc in next st, rep from * around, join with a sl st in beg ch.
* Continue to increase in this pattern, increasing 5 sts evenly spaced in each round, until the ball has the diameter you want.
* Now work as many rounds even in single crochet as you had increase rounds. For example, if you had 10 increase rounds,

work 10 rounds even in single crochet, without increasing or decreasing.
* Now decrease in the same pattern, decreasing 5 stitches evenly spaced around the piece. So if your last increase round was "sc in next 10 sts, 2 sc in next st," your first decrease round will be: Ch 1, *sc in next 10 sts, sc2tog, rep from * around, join with a sl st in beg ch.
* Continue to decrease in this pattern, with one fewer stitches between the decreases on every round. Stop when the ball is nearly done to stuff it with fiberfill, then continue decreasing, adding more stuffing as necessary as you finish the ball.
* When you have 5 stitches left, work one more round even, without decreasing. Fasten off, cut the yarn, weave the tail through the remaining stitches, and pull tight to close up the end of the ball.

Make the balls as small or as large as you want; just adjust the number of increase and decrease rounds. It is actually quite easy and really fun! It's almost addictive—just make sure you stop before your whole house is filled with colorful crochet balls!

There is something for everyone, and here the youngest in the family will have something nice and soft to squeeze. Not much can compare to a homemade teddy bear made by a close friend or relative. Here you can use your leftovers on something that will be highly appreciated!

Materials

* Pattern and tracing paper
* Fabrics
* Buttons
* Tailor's chalk
* Perle cotton
* Sewing needle
* Sewing thread
* Pins
* Sewing machine

Soft Teddy Bears for Little Ones

Sew on small buttons as eyes, or embroider them instead if the little one receiving this bear has a habit of stuffing everything in his or her mouth. A nose or a happy mouth in simple stitches is a cute detail. The girl bear has a heart in the middle of the belly, and the boy bear has a striped patch on the hip. Decorate your teddy bears so they have a personal touch.

DIRECTIONS:

* Transfer the pattern from the pattern sheet to tracing paper, and cut out.
* Draw the pattern parts on the fabric, add seam allowance, and cut out.
* Sew on the eyes and embroider the mouth and nose.
* Pin the pieces together and sew on a sewing machine. Leave an opening for reversing of a couple inches at the leg, where the seam is straight.
* Cut the seam allowance down and turn the teddy bear right side out. Make sure every corner is completely turned.
* Fill with fiberfill, and hand sew the opening closed with small stitches.

From the Kitchen

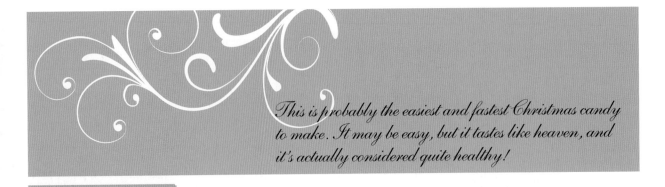

This is probably the easiest and fastest Christmas candy to make. It may be easy, but it tastes like heaven, and it's actually considered quite healthy!

Ingredients

* 7 oz. (200 g) dark chocolate
* 1¼ cup (3 dl) mixed nuts, such as pine nuts, cashews, almonds, and pistachios
* Orange zest

Tip
Treat yourself to a couple pieces before you put them out and the family starts digging in!

Chocolate with Nuts

These are fast and easy to make, and they disappear almost as quickly. You might as well double the recipe immediately!

I have used dark chocolate (70 percent or more), since it is the healthiest type, but you can use your own favorite chocolate. Use the nuts you like the most, together with almonds and the zest of an orange. Roasted nuts will contribute an extra-good taste, but they're not necessary. It is easy to melt chocolate in the microwave, and the result will be just as good as melting it in a double boiler.

DIRECTIONS:

* Chop the nuts and roast them fast in a frying pan with high heat until they are slightly golden colored.
* Clean the orange and zest with the finest side of the grater.
* Chop the chocolate in rough chunks and put them in a rather large bowl.
* Melt the chocolate in the microwave, 1 minute on high (for an 800-watt microwave). Take the bowl out and stir with a spoon. Put the bowl back in. The time can vary from half a minute to another minute. Take the bowl out and stir until all the chocolate has melted.
* Add the orange and nuts, and stir.
* Pour the mix out on parchment paper and smooth it out with a ladle or spatula.
* Leave the nut-chocolate to harden before you cut it into suitable pieces.

Christmas chocolates don't have to be complicated to taste good.

Ingredients

* ¾ cup (200 g) soft butter
* ¾ cup (2 dl) sugar
* 2½ cups (6 dl) oatmeal
* 2 tsp vanilla sugar (or you can substitute 2 tsp white sugar + ¼ tsp vanilla extract)
* 4 Tbsp cocoa powder
* 4 Tbsp mulled wine (alcoholic or non-alcoholic)

Topping:
* Corn flakes, sugar-coated corn flake cereal, or nib sugar

Candy Balls

Makes 30–40 candy balls.

This is a variant of the classic chocolate balls. The basic recipe is the one I use for chocolate balls the rest of the year, but for Christmas I use mulled wine as a flavoring. You can experiment and make up your own versions. For an extra-special look, serve them in small confectionery forms.

It's fastest to use a blender or a food processor to combine the ingredients; if you do, mix the oatmeal in at the end so that it does not get completely powdered. Then just start rolling!

Here I have used an alcoholic mulled wine, but that's not very child friendly. You can of course use non-alcoholic or make half of each.

DIRECTIONS:
* Mix all the ingredients in a bowl and stir until you have a moldable dough.
* Shape the balls in your palms. Try to make the balls the same size.
* Roll the balls in crushed cereal or pearl sugar.

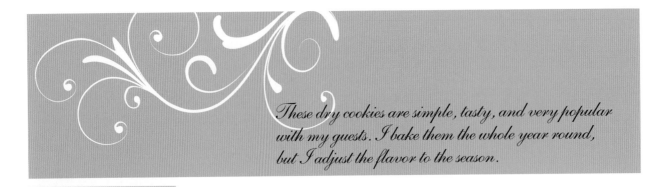

These dry cookies are simple, tasty, and very popular with my guests. I bake them the whole year round, but I adjust the flavor to the season.

Ingredients

* ½ cup (100 g) softened butter
* ¾ cup (2 dl) sugar
* 3 eggs
* 3 cups (7 dl) flour
* 3 tsp baking powder
* 1 tsp vanilla sugar (or you can substitute 1 tsp white sugar + ⅛ tsp vanilla extract)
* ½ teaspoon of salt
* 1 packet of saffron (0.5 gram)
* ⅓ cup (1 dl) raisins
* ⅔ cup (1½ dl) coarsely chopped almonds

Saffron Biscotti

Makes approximately 50 pieces. Bake at 350 degrees for about 15 minutes and allow time to dry.

It's nice to have a cookie jar for when unannounced guests decide to stop by. But it's unbelievable how fast these cookies disappear from the jar, sometimes without anyone knowing where they went . . . could it be the little angels of the house have been at work?

It's easy to vary the flavor of the biscotti. Switch out the almonds for walnuts, use cardamom instead of saffron, replace some of the flour with cocoa, and add lavender instead of raisins—the options are endless, and there is a flavor for everyone. It's important to leave the cookies in the oven until it is completely cold, to give them a chance to dry out. Then keep them in an airtight jar.

DIRECTIONS:

* Use a hand mixer to blend the butter and sugar until soft and airy.
* Add the eggs one by one while you continue to mix.
* Mix the dry ingredients together and then add them to the wet mix while you continue to mix.
* Place the dough on your counter and divide it into three parts.
* Roll each part out and put them on a baking sheet covered with parchment paper.
* Bake in the middle of the oven for about 15 minutes.
* Take out and cut the rolls diagonally until you have about 50 cookies.
* Turn off the oven and put the sheet with the cookies inside again. Leave them in the oven until it's completely cold.
* Store the cookies in an airtight box or jar.

Crisp bread is a very traditional Scandinavian food, dating back to 500 AD. These round wafers were made with a hole in the middle so they could be stored on sticks. Try out this easy and delicious treat this Christmas season!

Crisp Bread

Leave enough time for baking. You shouldn't be busy with something else, because this recipe takes time. It's a good idea to clear space in your kitchen before you start, because you need room for all the baking sheets . . . and also get a few extra baking sheets, as you'll need all you can get. I usually make a big pot of coffee and have a good book nearby, because there is a lot of waiting in between steps of this recipe. Meanwhile, my husband and our kids are anxiously peeking through the kitchen door, excited about the fresh crisp bread.

Makes 16 pieces of round crisp bread.

DIRECTIONS, DAY 1:

* Crumble the yeast in a mixing bowl and pour honey and salt over it.
* Add sour milk and water. The liquid should not be heated; add cold.
* Stir in rye and cover the bowl with plastic wrap. Leave it until the next day (you can leave for 24–30 hours).

DIRECTIONS, DAY 2:

* Crush the caraway in a mortar and put it in the dough.
* Add the barley and the whole wheat flour and lastly the regular flour.
* Stir well. Use a machine if you want.
* Put the dough out on your counter (flour the counter first), and divide into 16 pieces.
* Roll each piece into a little bun, and then roll it flat with a rolling pin. Turn often and use quite a lot of flour while rolling so the dough won't stick and break. Finish by rolling a patterned rolling pin over it. If you want, use a glass or something similar to make a hole in the middle.
* Put the pieces on a baking sheet and bake right away at 425 degrees for about 10 minutes.
* Remove the pieces from the oven and place on a cooling rack.
* Keep the crisp bread dry. You can line them up in a basket in a dry place.

Eat the crisp bread with a little butter and some delicious cheese. Yum!

Ingredients

DAY 1
* ½ package (25 g) cake yeast (or you can substitute 1 package/2¼ tsp dry yeast)
* 1 Tbsp honey
* 2 tsp salt
* ¾ cup (2 dl) sour milk
* 1⅔ cups (4 dl) water
* 2½ cups (6 dl) coarse rye flour

DAY 2
* 1¼ cups (3 dl) barley flour
* 1¼ cups (3 dl) whole wheat flour
* 1 Tbsp caraway seed
* 1 cup (2½ dl) white flour

Tip

I keep my crisp bread in a basket inside the oven, where it's nice and dry. I have made it a habit to look inside the oven before I turn it on, so the crisp bread won't bake another round.

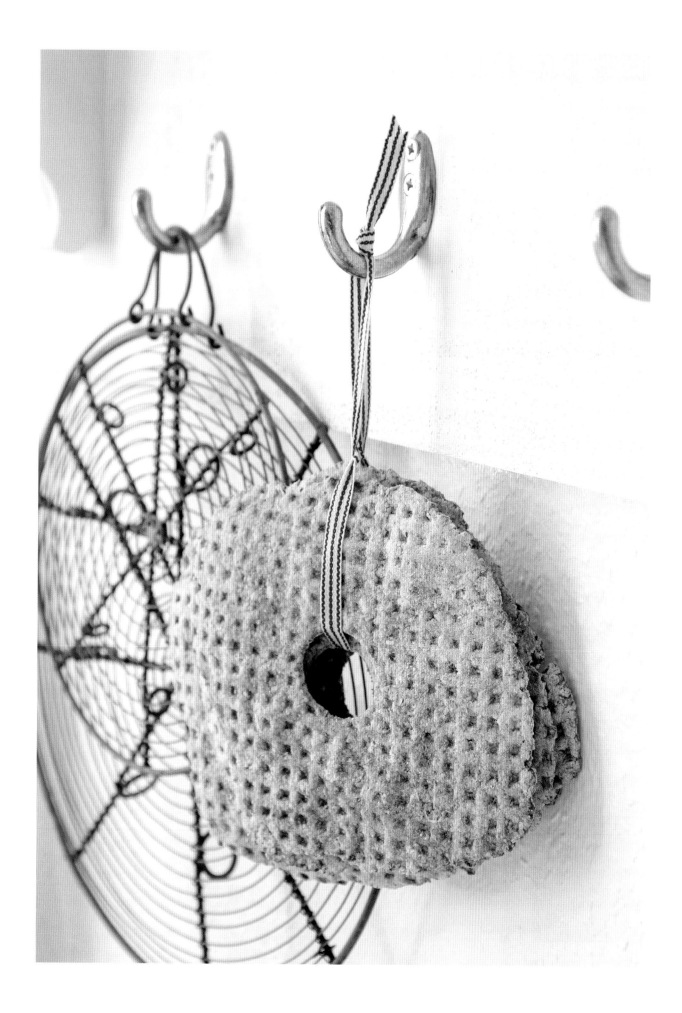

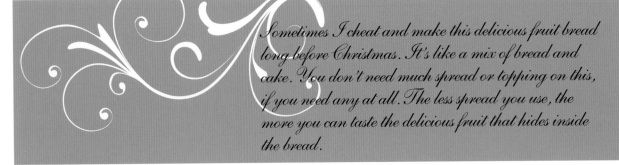

Sometimes I cheat and make this delicious fruit bread long before Christmas. It's like a mix of bread and cake. You don't need much spread or topping on this, if you need any at all. The less spread you use, the more you can taste the delicious fruit that hides inside the bread.

Delicious Fruit Bread

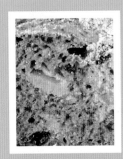

Ingredients

DAY 1
* ¼ package (12 g) cake yeast (or you can substitute ½ package/1 tsp dry yeast)
* 3 Tbsp honey
* 2 tsp salt
* 2½ cups (6 dl) lukewarm water
* 2 cups (5 dl) coarse rye flour

DAY 2
* ¾ cup (2 dl) flour
* 1⅔ cups (4 dl) whole wheat flour
* 1 Tbsp of cinnamon
* 3 tsp vanilla sugar (or you can substitute 3 tsp white sugar + ¼ tsp vanilla extract)
* 10 large dried seedless prunes
* 10 dried apricots
* 5 dried figs
* ⅓ cup (1 dl) raisins
* 1 cup (100 g) almonds

You can experiment with what you find in your cabinet. For example, I imagine dried pieces of apple would go well with these ingredients.

The baking is done over two days, but the dough mostly works on its own, so it's not too much work. And either way it's worth the work, because it tastes so good! Serve with butter and jam, or chutney or marmalade—along with a glass of sherry or mulled wine.

Bake in a 2-quart bread pan.

DIRECTIONS, DAY 1:
* Crumble the yeast in a mixing bowl and pour honey and salt over it.
* Heat the water to 100 degrees, stir the yeast mix with a little water, then add the rest of the water and stir.
* Stir in the rye and put plastic wrap over the bowl. Let it sit at room temperature until the next day.

DIRECTIONS, DAY 2:
* Stir flour into the dough and continue with the rest of the dry ingredients. You can use a food processor to mix the dough properly.
* Chop the fruits into smaller pieces, but leave the almonds whole. You do not have to blanche and peel them.
* Stir in the fruit and almonds and put the dough into the baking pan. Let the dough rise for about an hour.
* Bake the bread at the bottom of the oven at 400 degrees for about 70 minutes.
* Wrap the bread in double towels, place on a cooling rack, and leave it to cool. When it's cooled off you can move it over into double plastic bags. Let the bread sit for a couple of days before you eat it, but of course treat yourself with a taste first!

Patterns

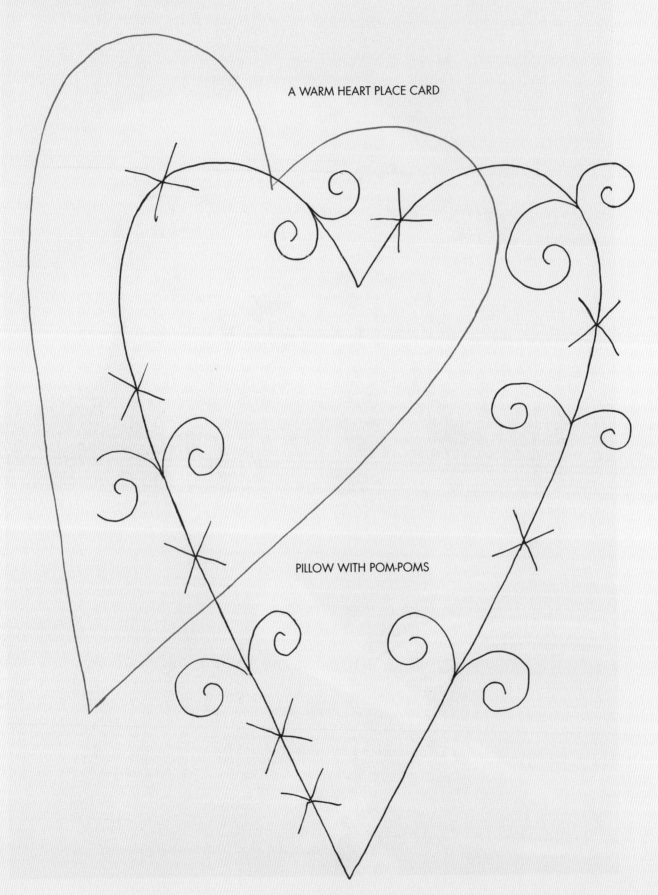

A WARM HEART PLACE CARD

PILLOW WITH POM-POMS

123
4567
890

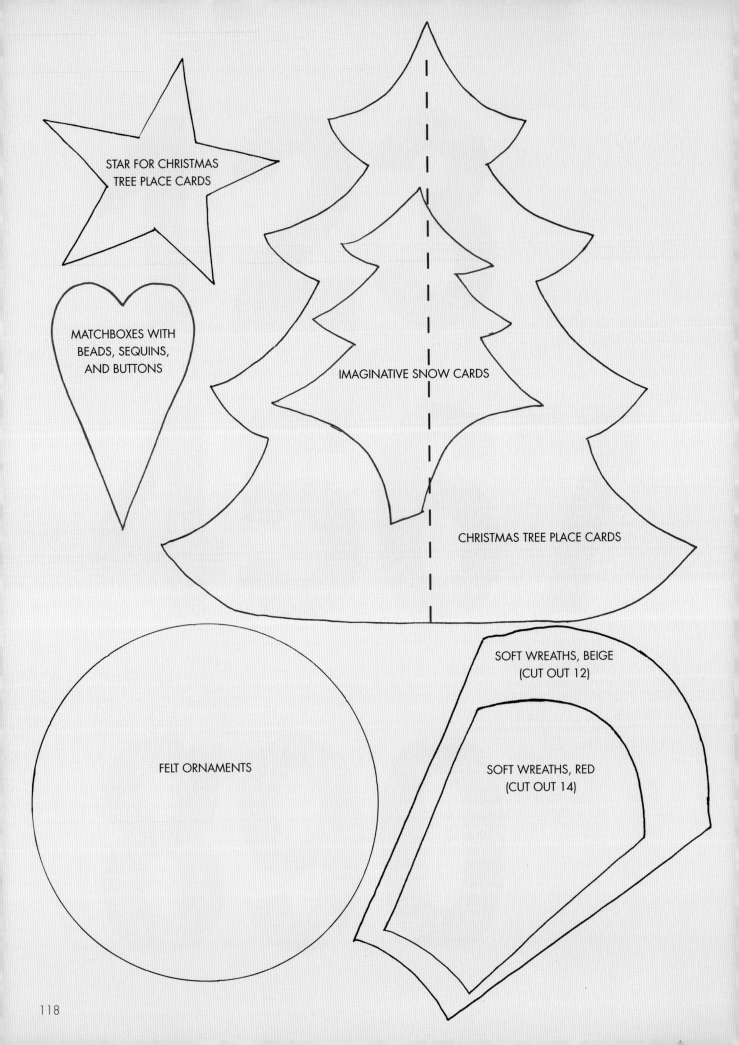

STAR FOR CHRISTMAS
TREE PLACE CARDS

MATCHBOXES WITH
BEADS, SEQUINS,
AND BUTTONS

IMAGINATIVE SNOW CARDS

CHRISTMAS TREE PLACE CARDS

SOFT WREATHS, BEIGE
(CUT OUT 12)

FELT ORNAMENTS

SOFT WREATHS, RED
(CUT OUT 14)

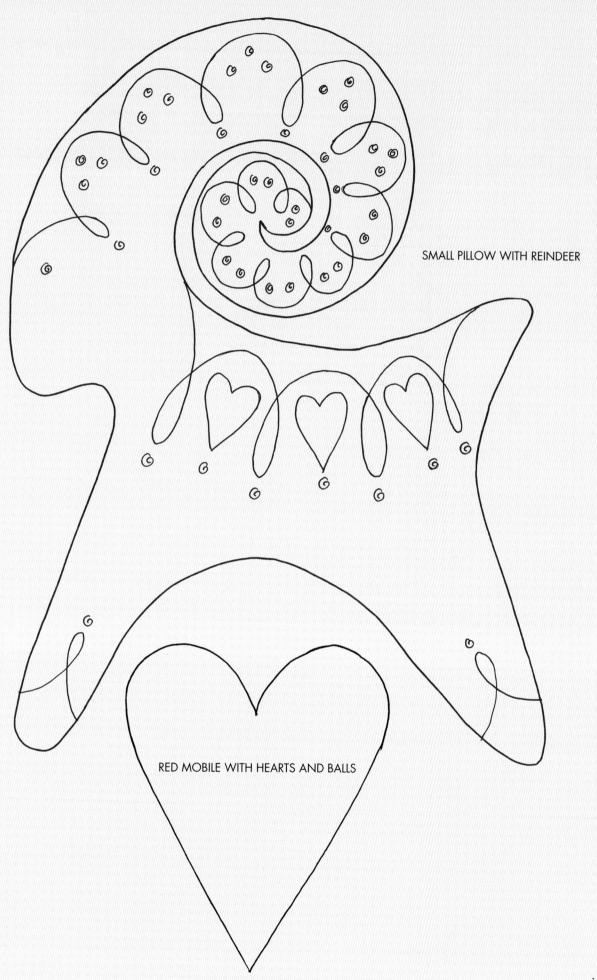

SMALL PILLOW WITH REINDEER

RED MOBILE WITH HEARTS AND BALLS

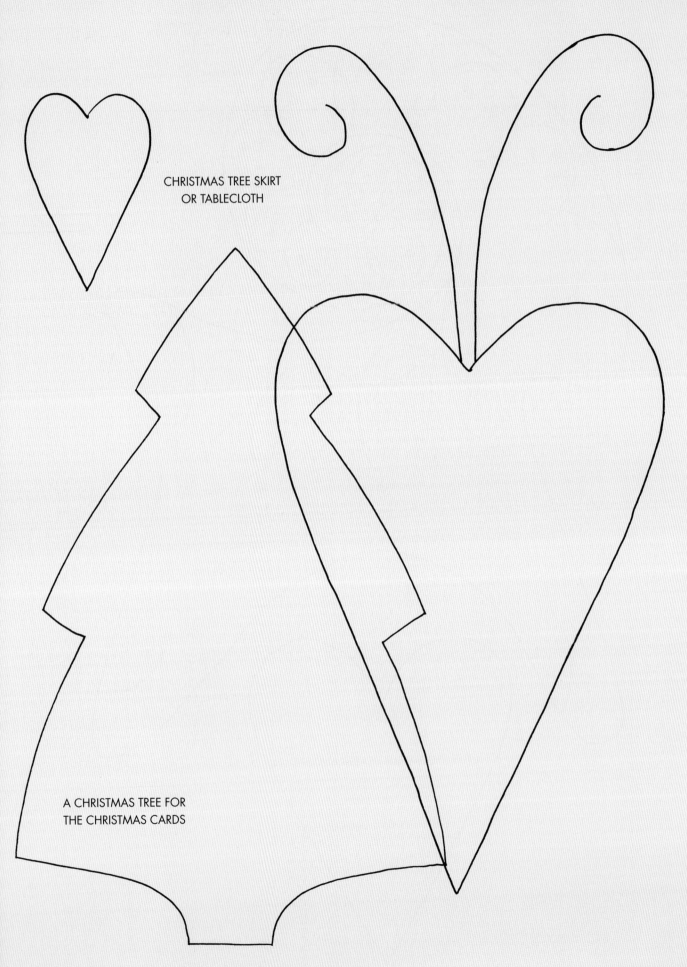

CHRISTMAS TREE SKIRT
OR TABLECLOTH

A CHRISTMAS TREE FOR
THE CHRISTMAS CARDS

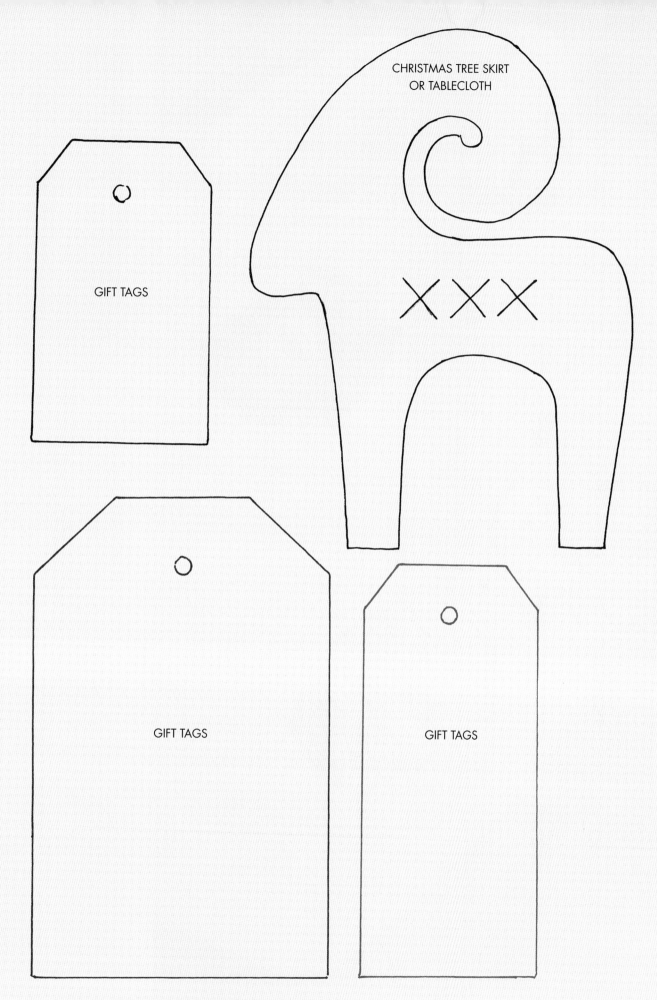

CHRISTMAS TREE SKIRT
OR TABLECLOTH

GIFT TAGS

GIFT TAGS

GIFT TAGS

121

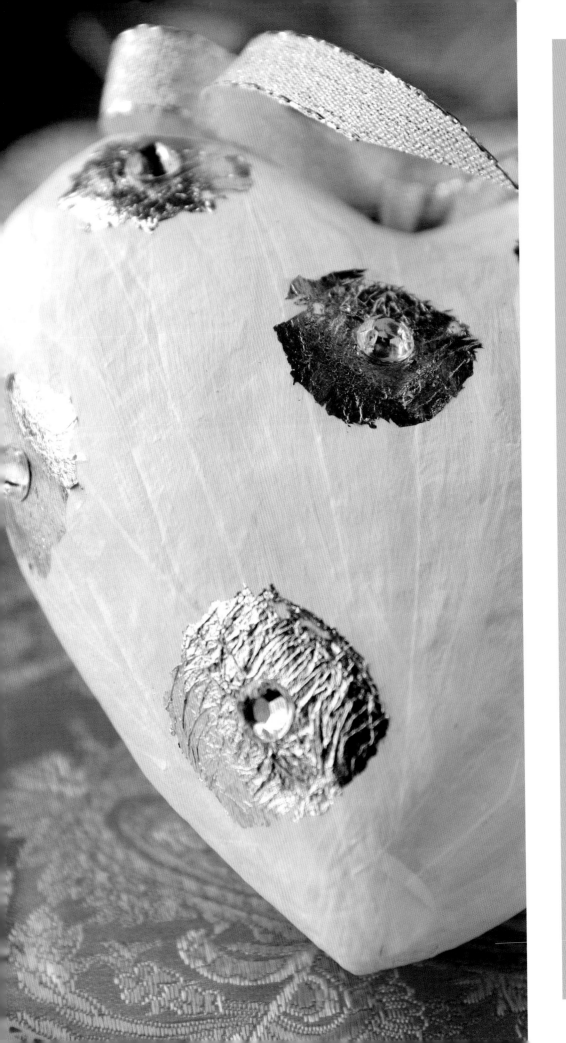

Leading the Way in Crafts

crochet for kids

Basic Techniques & Great Projects that Kids Can Make Themselves

Franziska Heidenreich

TUNISIAN CROCHET for BABY

Sharon Hernes Silverman

Crochet for Baby ALL YEAR

Easy-to-Make Outfits for Every Month
Tammy Hildebrand

Vintage Crochet Hats and Accessories

23 Classic Hats, Shawls, and Bags

Kathryn Fulton

crochet purses & accessories

Anne Rouzier & Vidian Uckardes

T-Shirt Yarn

PROJECTS TO CROCHET AND KNIT

Sandra Lebrun

KNITTING rugs

39 traditional, contemporary, innovative designs

Nola A. Heidbreder and Linda Pietz

knitted beanies & slouchy hats

31 original designs to suit your style & attitude

DIANE SERVISS

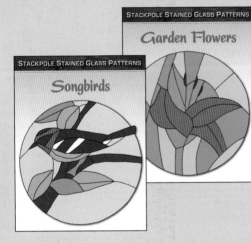

STACKPOLE STAINED GLASS PATTERNS

Songbirds

STACKPOLE STAINED GLASS PATTERNS

Garden Flowers

soy candles

How to Make Good-For-the-Earth, Long-Lasting Candles

Scandinavian CHRISTMAS CRAFTS and RECIPES

simply SAMPLERS

Easy Techniques for Hand Embroidery
a NeedleKnowledge book

Cheryl Fall

upcycled fashions for kids

31 cute outfits to create from found treasures
Cynthia Anderson

Smoking Food

A GUIDE TO SMOKING MEAT, FISH & SEAFOOD VEGETABLES, CHEESE, NUTS AND O

CHRIS FORTUNE

the KAMADO GRILL cookbook

150 Delicious Recipes for Foolproof Smoking, Grilling, and More

FRED THOMPSON

THE ULTIMATE DEHYDRATOR COOKBOOK

The Complete Guide to Drying Food, Plus 398 Recipes, Including Making Jerky, Fruit Leather, & Just-Add-Water Meals

Tammy Gangloff & September Ferguson

Avon Lake Public Library
32649 Electric Blvd.
Avon Lake, Ohio 44012

Discover inspiration and tips for your next project!
Scan to visit www.stackpolebooks.com to sign up for our e-newsletter
to receive exclusive discounts and free patterns.

11/14